FLATHEAD VALLEY

LANDMARKS

Historic Homes & Places of the Past

1st Edition

Written by Jaix Chaix

Edited By Kellyn Brown

First Printing: 2014

Published by WORD EXŌ INC.
PO BOX 502, Lakeside, MT 59922
wordexo.com

Cover and text design by Steve Larson of Flathead Beacon Creative, www.flatheadbeaconcreative.com

BOOK ORDERS:
Special discounts are available on quantity purchases by corporations, associations, educators and others. Please contact the publisher for discounts and details. U.S. trade bookstores and wholesalers please contact:

406-257-9220
billing@flatheadbeacon.com

ISBN 978-0-9903075-1-8

Cover photo credits: Courthouse by Lido Vizzutti, Polebridge Mercantile by Greg Lindstrom, all others by Jaix Chaix

Table of Contents

Foreword

In 2012, Jaix Chaix walked into our downtown Kalispell office. He had an idea. He wanted to write a weekly column focused on the history of the Flathead Valley – specifically, the landmarks that dot our region, the forgotten buildings we pass by on our commutes to work, from historic homes to dilapidated barns.

I was reluctant to offer him space, explaining how difficult it would be to come up with enough material worth telling a story about. He was persistent. We began running his column. And the response was immediate. Readers soon asked for him by name, although struggling with the pronunciation (it's "jay"). He led a bus tour through the city's historic neighborhoods and taught a course at the local community college.

Jaix proved me wrong; there are endless stories to tell. He also proved something else; his column, despite his initial pitch, isn't really about landmarks. At least, that's not why it resonates with me. Instead, it's about the people who lived here before us, who shaped this valley. When he tells a story about the unique characteristics of buildings, he's at once telling a story about the pioneers who laid their foundations.

For me, like many of our readers, "Landmarks" has become essential reading. This region's rural landscape is already widely appreciated. What Jaix provides is a thoughful appreciation of the nearer landscape that is so often overlooked.

Kellyn Brown, editor in chief, Flathead Beacon

Preface

This book is a collection of the initial fifty articles that were originally published in the "Landmarks" column of the Flathead Beacon newspaper between March, 2013 and April, 2014.

Admittedly, these articles offer just a glimpse of the people, places and architecture of bygone eras – and merely gloss the wide history of the Flathead Valley.

Consequently, this book hardly delves into the complex experiences of the people involved. And it barely mentions the architectural styles, influences and details that make these landmarks so culturally and architecturally significant.

Despite the shortcomings, it is hoped these articles can serve as "place-markers" – points of reference for revisiting the unique places and intriguing people of the past. And it is hoped this book inspires your imagination and encourages your interest in the history of the Flathead Valley and its unique places and people.

Jaix Chaix

Agather House

604 FIFTH AVENUE EAST, KALISPELL

WHILE THE ELEGANT, EARLY 20TH-CENTURY ARCHITECTURE OF the Agather House is plain to see, the history of the home may seem less obvious.

The home was built in 1910 for David Barber, a successful manager of the State Lumber Company – an enormous sawmill enterprise with unheard of production capacity, where more than 60 men could produce up to 500,000 board feet per day.

The working men about the mill had far more splinters in their hands than dollars. However, the investors and managers had none of the former, and plenty more of the latter (best measured in magnitudes). Indeed, successful management of such a mill yielded empire-starting rewards – and afforded Barber the opportunity to commission one of the finest architects available: Marion Riffo.

After selecting this suitable lot, which was then along the desirable outskirts of town, Barber and Riffo began designing the home. Riffo formed an indelible impression upon local architecture as he also designed the Kalispell Grand Hotel, St. Matthew's Church and other prominent homes and buildings in Kalispell. Riffo incorporated towering chimneys, a steep roof, a rolling porch, and other appointments into the home, which speak of the fine taste and grand design – yet also quietly bespeak tragedy.

Nobody could have predicted what happened to the Barber family (save for those with tarot cards, gypsy scarves, and the fortune of sheer coincidence). Tragically, by 1918, there would be nothing left of the Barber family, except for this house – all but empty except for sorrowful memories and fine furniture, hardly used.

The Barber family suffered a series of tragedies – the kind that sadden the heart and perplex courts with paperwork and precedents. The entire Barber family succumbed to complications borne of influenza and other afflictions that were the scourge of the era. While the front room was meant for entertaining, it was instead a quarantine for the sick and dying. Ultimately, nobody was left in the Barber family to claim ownership of the family possessions or the house.

Consequently, the house sat dormant for years. It was eerily desolate, save for the frightening thrashing noises heard inside the house. Some believed "souls were trapped inside its walls." And even some of the most rational folk, declared the house was haunted. That is, until it was discovered that barn swallows (not lost souls) had nested inside the walls and were responsible for all the noise.

In 1919, the home was cleared of court clerks and cobwebs and purchased by its namesakes: Alfons and Martha Agather. Alfons was born in Russia and served the imperial guard of Czar Nicholas there. As an immigrant in Kalispell, Alfons worked as the cashier and later president of the First National Bank of Kalispell (which was "the oldest bank in the Flathead County" even then).

With the roar of the early Twenties, it seemed prosperity and good fortune would prevail throughout the home, and with plenty of folly considering the flock of Agather children: Margaret, Veronica, Alfons, Victor, and Max.

Yet tragedy would strike again unexpectedly. Alfons died suddenly in 1929 (while visiting a sawmill in Washington), barely living a decade in the home.

The circumstances of Alfons' death caused Martha and daughter Margaret to renovate the home, so they could live in the basement and convert the rest of the home into several apartments. Their "apartment for rent" ads were staples of local newspaper classifieds from the 1930s until the late '50s.

Since then, the home has shaken the tragedies of its past. It now boasts a legacy of three generations that have adoringly cared for the home. Nikki Sliter is a present-day owner of the home. Incidentally, as a little girl, Nikki would walk by and tell her mom that she would live in the house someday – and now she actually does, along with her husband Everit.

Nikki keeps the home impeccably well – and adorns the home for Halloween, Christmas, and other occasions with striking decorations and flair.

Nowadays, the home is a neighborhood icon – a fun, family home festively decorated throughout the year (with memories of earlier tragedies tucked away in the original, built-in bookcases).

Anderson House

345 FIFTH AVENUE EAST, KALISPELL

THE YEAR 1908 WAS ONE OF MANY YEARS OF GRAND DEVELOPment in Kalispell and the surrounding area. It was the year when Henry Ford produced the first Model T automobile. Steamers plied the waters of Flathead Lake carrying passengers and towing timber and hay. And houses sprung up throughout burgeoning neighborhoods of Kalispell – including the one built on the corner lot at 345 Fifth Ave. E.

The house was built by Gilbert Ketcham, the principal of Flathead County High School from 1902 through 1911. It seems fitting that Ketcham, known for his love of teaching, would adopt the Craftsman style, which was not only an architectural style, but also a philosophy, if not a way of life.

The Craftsman style rebuked the overly decorated, ostentatious grandeur of the Victorian era. It paid homage to artisans and skilled workers who were seemingly made obsolete during the Industrial Revolution, and their know-how and fine craftsmanship (hence, the name).

And in many ways the Craftsman style – and the home itself – tells the story about how homebuilding was no longer an activity for the upper class, but the middle class as well. In retrospect, it seems unlikely that Ketcham, a man who loved teaching and sharing knowledge of language, science and the arts, would have chosen any other style for his home.

Ketcham lived in the home for just a few years after it was built. He sold it to Lloyd Shulkin, one of the five Shulkin brothers, who shared the home and operated a business together that sold clothes and gear to loggers in the area.

In 1918, the home was purchased by its namesake: Adolph Anderson, a Norwegian immigrant. And much like the practicality of the style of the home, Anderson lived in the home until his death in 1967, while the home remained in the family until 1980 (a legacy of more than 60 years).

While Adolph Anderson kept the same address, he certainly changed careers. While living in the home for nearly 50 years, he worked as a real estate agent, oil company manager, service station owner, and hotel keeper along with his sons at the Hotel Kalispell.

Today, many of the original style elements of the house are still plain to see. For example, there are vertical "blocks" of windows and other geometric design motifs (traceable to Frank Lloyd Wright, who greatly influenced the style). A gabled dormer, another signature of the Craftsman style, sits atop the side facing Fourth Street East. And white rafters and brackets beneath the blue eaves reinforce the decorative simplicity that is the mark of a Craftsman home.

The Craftsman style also plays with symmetry and numbers and this house has more than a few of these features. For example, there are four columns on the front porch. There are four steps to step inside the front door, which has four windows on each side. And the bay window has four panels – with four, scrolled brackets underneath.

In addition to what's on the outside, there are many stylistic elements inside the home, including arched entries between rooms, floor-to-ceiling kitchen cabinets, "lead windows," and the attractive heating registers at the floor.

Indeed, this home tells the story of the Craftsman style – not only by its design and construction, but also by its legacy of residents who in many ways embodied the Craftsman philosophy as well.

Anderson Style Shop

345 FIFTH AVENUE EAST, KALISPELL

DRIVING ALONG MAIN STREET IN KALISPELL IS MUCH LIKE DRIVING through history. And the building at 222 Main St. is just one of many that tells part of the history of business and commerce in downtown Kalispell.

In 1891, the Great Northern Railway chose Kalispell (instead of the now bygone town of Demersville) as the location for a division point. The decision sparked the birth of Kalispell, but sounded the death knell for Demersville. Consequently, many businesses and buildings moved from Demersville to Kalispell – literally, as many homes and buildings were relocated using horses, logs, and nearly every other necessary means.

The two-story building located at 222 Main St. was originally built in Demersville, about three miles away. It was first a grocery store and later the Pacific Union Tea Company. Around 1928, the address became known as the Anderson Style Shop. It was the namesake of its owner Carl Anderson, who founded the shop as the "headquarters for style and correctness" and "the newest, most modern ladies' ready-to-wear establishment" in Kalispell.

Anderson razed the original, wooden building in 1941. He then hired Fred Brinkman – perhaps Kalispell's most prominent architect – to redesign the building as a modern showcase of style.

Brinkman was noted as an architect who "influenced the physical appearance of his hometown more than any other single person." His designs shaped Kalispell from the 1920s to the 1950s. Notably, Brinkman also designed the Kalispell City Water Department Building, the Cornelius Hedges Elementary School, and nearly a dozen other buildings in Kalispell listed on the National Register of Historic Places.

Brinkman predominantly designed the building in "Style Moderne." The style shares common elements with "Art Deco," from which it partly evolved. It also shares elements with other contemporary styles such as "WPA Moderne," "Streamline Moderne," and "Nautical Moderne," as the sea horses flanking the crest near the roof line attest.

Various style elements and hints can be found throughout the building. Even a quick glance tells how this sleek, "streamlined" appearance (with no eaves, metal trim around the windows and doors, and light-colored façade) is from a quite different era of style and circumstance. For example, the top floor features metal-framed, block windows (Style Moderne) and streamlined, symmetrical lines (more Art Deco). The original second-story window also featured a lighted "Anderson's Style Shop" sign scripted across the entire area (the sign is gone, but the brackets are still visible). The bottom floor features asymmetrical lines with large, metal-framed windows that wrap around the entrance: a fusion of Style Moderne and Art Deco design elements.

The building is also perhaps a fusion and reflection of Brinkman's architectural style and personal life. For example, style elements of "WPA Moderne" can be found in the building. Incidentally, Brinkman, a former Army Corps of Engineers draftsman at the Panama Canal, served as chairman for the "decoration committee" for the local President's Ball

Committee in 1934 – a year before President Roosevelt established and appropriated the Works Progress Administration (WPA) in 1935 as part of his New Deal program.

The interior of the building was also notable. For example, newspaper articles featured the "Nairn Inlaid Linoleum," "Waterproof Tiling," and "Smith Broadloom Carpeting" flooring. And Miller-Ford Electric advertised, "The Last Word in Lighting Fluorescent" to describe their lighting installation in the shop, displayed on August 20, 1941 (just months before the Pearl Harbor Attack, and the United States joined World War II).

The Anderson Style Shop building later became known as Joyce's Style Shop, Ena's Clothing Store, Mimi's Bridal and Refinery, and Underground Books, depending upon who you ask, and which store they remember best.

Today, this landmark building is part of the Kalispell Main Street Historic District, and a unique example of Style Moderne in Northwest Montana.

Ant Flat Ranger Station

KOOTENAI NATIONAL FOREST

JUST SOUTH OF FORTINE, MONTANA YOU'LL FIND THE ANT FLAT Ranger Station. Initially, the site was part of the Lewis and Clark Forest Reserve, one of the oldest reserves in America. It was established in 1897 in honor of the Lewis and Clark Expedition that passed through the area between 1804 and 1806.

However, even though presidential proclamations established the reserve, little was known about the area. For most American settlers, the area was a vast, unmapped wilderness that had been mostly unexplored since the initial Lewis and Clark Expedition itself.

In 1902, President Theodore Roosevelt commissioned his friend, fellow hunter, and fellow Rough Rider Fred Herrig to find an ideal location for a ranger station. He decided to settle and establish the station – in the same area where it is today – since it was a vast meadow with a good source of water.

Prior to his sojourn, Herrig made many preparations. President Roosevelt gave his saddle to Herrig for the journey (the very saddle can be seen at the Miracle of America Museum in Polson, Montana). And along with his black horse and Russian wolfhound, Herrig also brought along many provisions – including lilac bushes.

It seems Herrig had intended to plant the lilac bushes and name the station "Lilac Hall." However, despite Herrig's lilac-laden intentions, his friend and crew-member Byron Henning noticed all the "gol-durned ant hills in the meadow" and mockingly advocated that the name "Ant Flat" was far more appropriate. The name stuck and Herrig became the first ranger of the Ant Flat Ranger Station.

Incidentally, while the name "Lilac Hall" didn't stick, and the original buildings that Herrig and his crew had built are long gone, lilac bushes from the ones Herrig first planted are still on the property. So Herrig's legacy of lilacs does carry on.

Herrig and his crew established the ranger station at a time when "Fortine" was little more than a settlement. The post office named in honor of early settler Octave Fortin was not established until 1905 (land records from 1892 bear the name Octave Fortin – without the "e" at the end). And the bustling logging operations and clamor at the Fortine depot did not get underway until about 1906.

Even then, the area was sparse. Joseph Gussenhoven, who established logging operations near the Ant Flat Ranger Station, reported in 1907 that despite his success, and the Great Northern buying the entire output of his sawmill, he nonetheless had "great trouble keeping his mills in operation through the scarcity of labor" in the area.

And while Ant Flat Ranger Station offered access to the railroad and to Brimstone Creek, it also offered relative isolation and other hardships that Herrig and his crew had to overcome. But they persevered and established the ranger station, which operated from 1902 until 1963.

Unfortunately, the original buildings on the site are gone and were burned to make way for the "newer" buildings that stand today. The green garage and mechanic's shop were built in 1932. The "white house" with a gambrel roof was built in 1922. Originally, it served as a warehouse, but was later converted into a ranger's office.

The log-built barn that still stands on the property was begun in 1921 and completed in 1925. And a closer and careful look around the barn, reveals how some of the iron and steel hardware seems hand-forged.

Today, the station is part of the Kootenai National Forest and an historic site, nature trail and environmental education center. Visiting the site and walking the Ant Flat Nature Trail is good for enjoying nature – and just as good for getting lost back in time.

Baldwin House

428 THIRD AVENUE EAST, KALISPELL

SOME HISTORIC HOMES MAY NOT SEEM AS BOLD OR STRIKING ON the outside – but nonetheless have a profound history on the inside. The "Baldwin House" is perhaps one of those homes, as its rather modest exterior, partially hidden behind the shrubbery, disguises the rich history of the home.

Indeed, some may have noticed this house, perhaps for its gabled roofs at the front and sides, and have easily overlooked the remarkable history about the family that once lived here for generations.

The home is one of Kalispell's first and was built in 1891 – the same year the town of Kalispell was established and platted. And for eighty-two years, the home remained in the Baldwin family.

The home was originally built for Major Marcus Dana Baldwin and his family. Before they moved into the home, Baldwin was appointed by President Grover Cleveland as an agent of the Peigan, Káínaa ("Bloods"), and the Siksikáwa ("Blackfoot") bands on the Blackfeet Indian Reservation.

Baldwin and his wife Sarah had two boys before they lived on the Blackfeet reservation. And they had a daughter while they lived on the reservation – the first "white person" to be born on the Blackfeet Indian Reservation. When the tribal elders first saw Baldwin's daughter – they exclaimed "Kokoa!"(which means "little girl" in the Blackfeet language).

The name Kokoa stuck, and Kokoa Baldwin was so named by the prominent tribal members Two Guns White Calf, Little Dog, Big Nose, and Little Plume, who are all historical figures in their own right. Perhaps the most well-known is Chief Two Guns White Calf, whose face and likeness was used for the portrait on the back of every "Indian Head" nickel, or "Buffalo Head" nickel as it is also known.

After serving on the reservation, Baldwin and his family moved to Demersville in 1889. A year later, with the "Demise of Demersville," the Baldwin family moved once again to Kalispell and settled in this house. Baldwin then began to establish himself as one of Kalispell's first prominent attorneys.

In 1892, the Baldwin sons Mark and Phil, left boarding school in Grand Rapids, Mich., and rejoined the family under the same roof of the home. Mark served in the First Montana Infantry, Company II, during the Spanish War. And Phil moved to the Philippine Islands and worked as a customs agent. Their younger brother, Charles, served in World War I.

The Baldwin family shared some admirable traits as generations of the family had served their country in one capacity or another. Father Marcus Baldwin was regarded as an excellent swimmer and marksman – as was his daughter Kokoa. And the entire Baldwin family seemed to share an appreciation for the outdoors (perhaps stemming from Marcus' superior outdoor skills which helped establish Marias Pass for use by the Great Northern Railway).

Unfortunately, for Kokoa, love for the outdoors was not only a passion, but part of her fate. Kokoa died in 1932, after succumbing to injuries she sustained while skiing on New Year's Day (Kokoa was interned next to her father Marcus at the Conrad Cemetery).

Coincidentally, Kokoa had a son named Charles, who died several years before – also on New Year's Day. The elder Kokoa Baldwin also had a daughter, who was named Kokoa as well. The younger Kokoa carried on the legacy of the name after her mother died, and took care of the home as well.

Originally, the home was only a humble one-story brick structure with a gabled roof. Around 1914, the home was remodeled and a second story with wood framing and another gabled roof were added. The area at the back of the home was added to the original brick structure much more recently.

The carriage house at the alley also reveals some history as well. Construction of the carriage house began in 1899 and it was completed in 1903. The outline of the carriage house reveals how it was intended to accommodate little more than a horse and carriage (as daily use of an automobile was hardly an idea at the time).

So if you're walking along Third Avenue in Kalispell, stop for a moment to appreciate this home – not only for the early, original architecture on the outside, but for the rich family history on the inside.

Dr. Albert Brassett Residence

628 FOURTH AVENUE EAST, KALISPELL

THE HOME AT 628 FOURTH AVE. E. REPRESENTS SOME LONG TRADITIONS of Kalispell's past.

For starters, this grand home is a hallmark of the "Kalispell Craftsman" style and an epitome of popular architecture in its day. The home was designed by architect Marion Riffio, who greatly influenced the architectural landscape of Kalispell.

Aside from the house, Riffio also designed the Kalispell Grand Hotel (the only one of many original hotels left in town), the Liberty Theatre and many homes in the Kalispell area (even churches as far as Havre). The history of Riffio's designs include this house – and a distinct mark on the Craftsman style in Kalispell.

The house also represents another long-lasting tradition: the Dr. Albert Brassett family. The Brassetts lived in the home for forty-five years until their passing. And for more than three generations, Albert Brassett served as a family physician in the Flathead Valley.

Albert was born in Trondheim, Norway. As one of six children, he was "farmed out" of school to work on the family plot. Consequently, he did much farming, and little learning. He moved to the United States and out of steerage when he was thirteen.

After making up for the education he had missed, Brassett returned to school, and then attended college and medical school. Afterward, he married his wife, Minnie (née Larsen).

Together they left St. Paul, Minnesota, and arrived in Kalispell on July 4, 1909.

When the Brassetts arrived in Kalispell, Albert "hung a shingle" and began practicing medicine. And a couple of years later, Minnie's father offered a rather tidy marriage dowry – this house.

And while the home represents the distinct Craftsman style, it also played an important role in another tradition (somewhat more difficult to recognize): the home was one of the first homes in Kalispell with an automobile.

Before 1913, Brassett walked to his house calls and rented a horse and buggy to reach the homes and farms that were beyond town. Brassett was a pioneer of sorts, as he embraced the idea of using an automobile to make house calls even though popular opinion – and the opinion of even some auto manufacturers – held that a doctor would be better served with a horse and carriage when responding to an emergency.

The house was relatively close to the Kalispell General Hospital, where Brassett performed the very first surgery (actually, twice). He technically performed the very first surgery at Kalispell General. And when a larger operating room was added in 1949, Brassett was also given the honor of performing the first surgery again (in the new, larger operating room).

The Brassetts lived in the house for more than forty-five years and raised two children, Sylvia and Arnold, in the home. Unfortunately, Minnie passed in 1952, while Albert did not retire until 1954, on his 80th birthday. He passed away at the home in 1956.

The home has many appointments inspired by sensible design and pleasing aesthetics. For example, the home offered a design and layout that embraced casual living (and more than a few competitive bridge games that the Brassetts were known for hosting).

The full front porch also has a dormer porch at the top. Along with the decorative wood trim, wide roof eaves, and decorative windows, the home also features a flared-brick chimney and both shingle and narrow, clapboard siding.

And aside from its hallmarks of the Craftsman style, the house was known for its long-standing tradition as the home of Dr. Albert Brassett – the doctor who served patients throughout the Kalispell area for decades.

Brintnall House

321 FIFTH AVENUE EAST, KALISPELL

IN 1894, KALISPELL WAS STILL QUITE A SPARSE TOWN. THE CITY was only two years old and still burgeoning as a place of industry, where railroading and farming, and sawmills and flourmills coalesced.

It was the same year in which Reverend Olin Wesley Mintzer bought one of the original town sites from Charles E. Conrad's Kalispell Townsite Company. Mintzer built a home for himself here, at 321 Fifth Avenue East, in the popular Queen-Anne style.

Newspapers of yesteryear are full of articles noting the Methodist Episcopal Reverend Mintzer officiating marriages at various homes and churches. However, Mintzer's residence in this home did not last long. In 1896, he was appointed to another church in Great Falls and moved there.

Despite the brief residency of Reverend Mintzer and his family, his choices constructing the home would last more than a century. For example, the home has gabled roofs on all sides, often called a cross-gabled roof. And like many folks in the late nineteenth century, Mintzer opted to construct the home with wood framing with decorative siding, typical of the day (despite the value and availability of local-fired brick). The Mintzers' preference for ornate stained-glass windows, patterned siding, and fanciful scroll work have also outlasted generations and remain part of the house today.

After the Mintzer's ownership, the home would establish a long and important history of residents and ownership – well worth noting.

In the early 1900s, Frederick French and his family lived in the home. In addition to his success as the proprietor of American Steam Laundry, French also rented the home to eight boarders. French had a unique amenity when it came to advertising rooms for rent. His American Steam Laundry company handled laundry from towns as far away as Libby and Roundup – and also provided laundry service for boarders who rented a room in the house.

After the French family resided here, the home was owned by its namesake, Chester C. (Chet) Brintnall. Brintnall served the local postal service from 1902 until 1948 – almost forty-six years of service. When Brintnall started as a mail clerk in 1902, Kalispell had no parcel post delivery, no delivery in the city, and no rural delivery either – just a general delivery window. Brintnall witnessed many changes in postal service and the town of Kalispell itself before he retired in 1948 as assistant postmaster, the position he held since 1916.

In 1923, Brintnall made the home even more noteworthy as he leased it to Frank Bird Linderman: also known as "Sign Talker," or former Montana Assistant Secretary of State Linderman, or state legislator Linderman – and perhaps most well-known of them all, Linderman the famous Montana author.

Linderman moved to Montana Territory in 1885 at the age of 16 as a trapper and pioneer. He lived and learned among the Native Americans along the shores of Flathead Lake near

Bigfork and Lakeside and mastered their sign language (earning him the name Sign Talker).

By 1923, Linderman had already published several written works. Linderman bought the Kalispell Hotel as part of his plan to earn enough money to later finance his writing career. While running the hotel, Linderman lived here, in the Brintnall residence.

While the home does not bear Linderman's name, a Kalispell school building is named after him, and so is an elementary school in Polson. Indeed, this house played a critical, yet quiet role in the life of one of Montana's famous writers (which you could hardly guess from walking or driving past the outside).

Since Linderman's residency, the house has been exceptionally well maintained. Maybe the care and maintenance was born of pride of ownership, or perhaps from well-minded intentions to preserve the rich, important history of the home – one that played a pivotal role in Montana's literary history at the least.

Bruyer Granary

1355 WHITEFISH STAGE ROAD, KALISPELL

ALONG WHITEFISH STAGE ROAD IN KALISPELL, A LOST TYPE OF architecture – and way of life – has been well preserved.

The yellow, square barn with "1909" on the side of it is actually a granary that was built to store grain on the Kal-Mont dairy farm (abbreviated from "Kalispell, Montana"). Although the Kal-Mont dairy farm was once about 440 acres, little is left of this hard-working farm, except for the granary and its surrounding area, as the rest of the acreage has been developed. And while there are many granaries throughout the Flathead Valley, the Bruyer Granary is a fine example of an early 20th-century "cribbed" granary.

The granary was built by the Bruyer family: Julius Bruyer and his sons Philip, Lawrence, Elmer and Nickolas. Julius Bruyer was originally born in France in 1853. He immigrated to America with his family a few years later. He later married Susanna Birgen in 1883. Together, they initially worked a family farm in South Dakota.

In 1901, they moved to Kalispell – which had plenty to offer since it was the county seat, a center of the timber industry, and a railroad division point which offered access to plenty of markets both near and far.

And while the granary shows the fine workmanship of the Bruyer family, it also shows the hope and optimism they had for their future. For example, the granary is a scaled-down version of the large, commercial grain elevators along the Great Lakes and railroad tracks throughout the plains.

Aside from being a "miniature" of something much bigger, the Bruyer Granary was built to hold up to 11,000 bushels – which clearly evidences the success they planned for their farm. Also in considering the sentiment of the era, it was hard not to be optimistic as Flathead County doubled in population between 1900 and 1910.

The construction of the Bruyer Granary is also quite unique. It was built using the "cribbing" method. That is, pieces of wood, one for each side, were laid flat to make a square. These formed squares were then stacked on top of each other to build up the walls (much like stacking logs to build up the side of a log cabin). Once tall enough, the square formation was then sided to keep its strength and form.

The granary also shows that the Bruyer family had ingenuity – a factor that often made the difference between a successful farm, and one that would soon be sold. For example, the Bruyers built the granary so that a wagon loaded with grain bushels could drive alongside it. Then, using a hand-cranking system that they devised themselves, the loaded wagon could be lifted to the second story of the granary. While raised, the bushels on the wagon were then unloaded into the bins below. After unloading the bushels, the empty wagon was lowered down to the ground on the other side of the granary (this way, one wagon could be lowered, while another was being lifted).

The granary has passed hands over the years, to son Nickolas Bruyer, and later the Schulze family, who purchased the property in 1950. Fortunately (and most thankfully) the Schulze family generously donated the granary and the land surrounding it to the City of Kalispell for historic preservation.

Incidentally, Carl Naumann and his wife Ellen (née Bruyer), a granddaughter of Julius Bruyer, helped restore the granary so residents and visitors could appreciate it.

So the next time you travel along Whitefish Stage Road in Kalispell, and pass a granary with "1909" on its side, realize that you're passing a historic landmark – one that is rich in agricultural history, ingenuity, self-sufficiency, and a bygone way of life.

Catholic Parish/Bjorneby House

435 FOURTH AVENUE EAST, KALISPELL

THE HOME AT 435 FOURTH AVENUE EAST WAS ONE OF KALISPELL'S original brick-clad, American Foursquare style homes (of which relatively few remain intact).

When it was originally built, sometime before 1897, the American Foursquare style was rising to popularity. It was a style that had much in common with Prairie and Craftsman architectural styles – and had little to do with the ornate ambitions of the Victorian era.

Early on, the house served as the parsonage for the St. Matthew's Catholic Church. And between 1907 and 1925 it was the home of Kalispell's longtime Catholic priest Francis X. O'Farrell (who was born in Woodford, County Galway, Ireland in 1865).

While living in the home, O'Farrell was managing the building of St. Matthew's Catholic hospital, parochial school, and a "newer" brick church five blocks to the west (the old Catholic church once stood next door to this house).

After serving the parish, the home began its secular life when Emil Gunneriusson Bjorneby, son of Norwegian immigrants purchased the home in 1928. Before Emil and his wife Margaret moved in, they transformed the modest Foursquare into the fashionable Tudor Revival house it is today (although the original brick carriage house at the alley reveals a glimpse of how the house originally looked, as both the house and the carriage house once looked the same).

The Bjorneby family arrived in Kalispell in 1895. Mary Bjorneby raised their five daughters, while her husband Emil worked in a hardware store, and then involved himself in groceries, farming and real estate, before founding the Bjorneby Flour Mill with his brother George in 1909.

If the name Bjorneby Flour does not seem familiar anymore, then perhaps the name Emil Bjorneby may be familiar as he served five terms in the Montana Legislature. Bjorneby began his political career in 1932 while still living in the house (the same year a large fire unfortunately ravaged the flour mill).

Aside from keeping a long political career, Emil Bjorneby kept a long marriage, as the Bjornebys were married sixty-two years. He was also a resident of the same block on Fourth Avenue East for fifty-four years (Bjorneby first lived at 435 Fourth Avenue East, and then moved next door at 445, after building a new home where the old church once stood).

Fortunately, many of the stylistic changes Bjorneby made in the late 1920s are still visible today. For example, the half-timbered gable at the second floor is a hallmark of the Tudor-Revival style. So are the long, multi-paned windows, the tall, obvious chimney and the whimsical slopes and curves of the rooflines on the covered front and side porches.

Aside from the style of the home, it should be appreciated for its role in early Kalispell history (both for when it was originally built and when it was remodeled during the "transforming twenties" in Kalispell). It should also be appreciated for how its original bricks still stand behind its stucco facade, and are still part of the old carriage house at the alley. And last, but not least, the house should be appreciated as a home to one of Kalispell's early prominent families and its namesake: the Bjorneby family.

City Water Department

312 FIRST AVENUE EAST, KALISPELL

IT MAY SEEM A LITTLE ODD THAT THE KALISPELL CITY WATER Department building is listed on the National Register of Historic Places. But odd is OK. Especially since this fine example of Georgian Revival architecture is a landmark in its own right – and one with a fascinating trove of "underground history."

Installing water mains and water pipes was an early business in Kalispell, and about as old as the town site itself.

On January 1, 1892, the first Great Northern Railway locomotive pulled into Kalispell. To commemorate the occasion and herald the progress of the era, local gunsmith George Stannard made a silver railroad spike out of melted silver dollars. The spike was set near Main Street and first struck by Mrs. Mary Kimmerly. The spike was then driven by one of the earliest pioneers of the Flathead Valley, Nick Moon (incidentally, Moon once lived in one of the earliest homesteads in the Flathead Valley, but moved away shortly after this commemoration as he felt things had become much "too civilized" for life in the 1890s).

As the first train pulled out, and the soot settled, the business of water works was well underway. And by the mid-1890s, a couple of outfits held the market on the water main business in Kalispell. Coincidentally, this was about the same time of another transportation "fad": bicycling, or "scorching" (according to those who complained of the incredible speeds at which people pedaled along the wooden plank sidewalks through town). And as the "scorched" sidewalks and muddy streets would be improved above, so too would the water mains and water pipes below.

By 1913, supplying water to homes in Kalispell became a municipal service, and no longer a free enterprise for the likes of Kalispell Water & Electric Co. or the Northern Idaho & Montana Power Co. (NIM&H). And William H. Lawrence, a former construction supervisor for NIM&H Power Co., began working for the city of Kalispell, and helped established the City Water Department.

In his transition to a municipal supervisor, Lawrence would serve as a rare blend of able manager and concerned advocate. He supervised the installation and maintenance of more than twenty miles of water mains and water connections throughout the city – and he would also forge an historical and architectural legacy.

Historically, it seems Lawrence preferred fastidious record keeping. Subsequently, he insisted that water department records be compiled into annual reports. These reports, dating back to 1913, include details and photographs of the earliest buildings and streets in Kalispell – and many shown in their long-forgotten, original form. Poring over these reports reveals a unique "underground" history of Kalispell.

Aside from good record-keeping, Lawrence was also responsible for the solid construction of "a new building" for the water department offices. He collaborated with local, renowned architect Fred Brinkman to forge a rather unique design for a municipal building. And in 1927, many local craftsman helped realize their design and complete the City Water Department building.

Some of the unique features of the building include the arched windows, Corinthian capitals on the door pilasters, and a bracketed cornice. These and other architectural details should seem even more unique, considering that the City Water Department is the only municipal building of its era that remains standing.

The old City Jail, which once stood to the south of the Water Department, was converted (ironically, to a brothel at one point) and the new structure there today bears no historical resemblance to the original whatsoever. Likewise, the old City Hall that was built in 1904 and adjoined the Water Department to the north was demolished in 1981.

So while nearly every original municipal building of the era has been dramatically altered or demolished, the City Water Department building remains – with much of its original character and historical legacy all its own.

F.W. Cole House

503 FIFTH AVENUE EAST, KALISPELL

THE HOUSE AT 503 FIFTH AVENUE EAST IN KALISPELL PROVES THAT wonderful homes come in many shapes, styles and forms. At first glance, the home is obviously a Cape; or is it a refined Foursquare? No matter its form, it is clearly appointed in the Queen Anne style; or is it a partially remodeled Tudor?

Casting definitions aside, here's what the house really is: a proud blend of forms and styles that were popular in the early 20th century. And it's a fine example of what any good home should do: suit the fancy of its owners and delight its neighbors.

The home was designed by Frank W. Cole, who laid the blueprints and built the house himself, so both he and his wife, and later their daughter Dorothy Ann, could live there. And live there they did, for more than 40 years until 1975.

The precise style of the home may seem peculiar. And it was just as peculiar when the house was built in 1932 – a time when the effects of the Great Depression were still manifest, and "recovery" would not actually begin in earnest until a year later.

Undoubtedly, building a home like this – at a time like this – takes more than your average moxie. And Cole certainly seemed to have plenty of the kind earned the hard way. He founded Cole's Machine Works with his father, Frank G. Cole, former manager of Kalispell Iron Works. They founded their company in 1928, barely a year before Black Tuesday, the stock market crash of Oct. 29, 1929, which often marks the start of the Great Depression.

And likely through perseverance (and much hard work) the Cole's shop at 217 First Ave. W. (reached by phone by dialing 1-8-0) kept them busy, and spared them from "the breadline." Together, the father and son team were dealers in iron, steel, brass and aluminum castings and sash weights (window technology had yet to develop beyond counter-weights at the time).

Newspaper advertisements in the early 1930s reveal their relative success. And they also show that Cole's handiwork at the lathe, albeit crafting saw arbors, barrel stoves, grate bars, and other matters of metal and precision, would soon be applied to the wood and windows about his home with similar craft and precision.

The craftsmanship of the Cole House, inside and out, is impeccable. And while unique for its appearance, the home is also unique for its circumstances. It was built by a successful local craftsman, in the thick of tough times, by himself, for himself and his family – and kept proper by the same hands and care for decades. Homes of such kind are rare, no matter where they stand.

Even more rare, is such a home that is as delightful as it is precise – a house that can make you smile as you walk past, no matter the season, nor weather. The large windows with fanciful scroll-work, the ever-so-narrow windows flanking the front door, the bright colors define the house – and defy frowns. Both Mr. and Mrs. Cole were civic-minded, and members of various local organizations, and often entertained family, friends, and guests at the home. And these appointments likely inspired a cheery atmosphere for guests and visitors, before they even crossed the transom.

The F. W. Cole House is a fine example of how different forms and styles, borne of eclecticism and personality as much as craftsmanship, can mix. It also provides an important reminder about appreciating any historic home: enjoy it for what it is – whatever that may be.

Conlon House

604 FOURTH AVENUE EAST, KALISPELL

INDEED, PINK HOUSES ARE PRETTY MUCH A LANDMARK DUE TO their color alone. But stately, historic pink houses are in a league all their own.

The grand home at 305 Fourth Ave. E. was built by James Conlon, who took over the bankrupt Kalispell Mercantile, and reaped much success. Conlon intended the home as a gift for his wife Mary. He commissioned architect Joseph B. Gibson to render the design and contractor George F. Simmonds to build upon the plans.

Conlon's fine taste and Gibson's exceptional appointments produced nothing short of an iconic, 19th-century mansion in Georgian Revival style. And with just a blush, the home's classic appointments are abundantly obvious, such as the portico at the middle of the roof, the balusters, dentil work, quoins (the "blocks" along the corners), chimneys at both sides, and many other aspects that helped define this strictly symmetrical style.

And if the radial entryway with its Ionic columns did not signify elegance, the porte-cochère at the side of the house certainly provided for any missing emphasis. This covered side entrance allowed occupants of horse and carriage buggies (and later automobiles) to alight and enter the home without any regard for the weather, which was truly a grand social statement of the era.

The interior of the home was spared little of high style as well, with the leaded glass windows set in mahogany, the oak woodwork in the library, the mahogany used in a second-floor bedroom, and the other exotic woods and finished throughout the home.

These appointments were not just for decoration, but for durability, which was a consideration throughout the home.

While most of the rooms inside the home may seem typical (bedroom, kitchen, dining room) the house features a type of room that is quite a rarity these days: a fernery – a room devoted specifically for growing and showcasing ferns (and often other exotic plants).

Conlon and Gibson also applied some ingenuity throughout the home as well. For example, a radiator in the dining room featured a built-in food warmer to help keep food warm during dinner service.

And to dull the labor of getting wood to the fireplace, a fanciful seat in the hallway is actually a cover for a woodbox on a dumbwaiter. This allowed for firewood to be stacked inside the box in the basement, and drawn on the dumbwaiter up to the main floor.

The Conlon House, with its iconic grandeur, was later nicknamed "The Embassy" by adoring neighbors. It is quite a fitting moniker, considering all of the tea parties, socials and other events that were held in the home. Quite often "reception committees" would receive 50 or more guests at the home, including some of the most influential people of the day.

In 1945, much like James Conlon, Mr. B.M. Wohlwend bought the home as a gift for his wife Jennie and their daughter, Lois. The home was passed on and later became the home of Lois, her husband and former Montana state Sen. Matt Himsl, and their children.

And while many homes of this stature tend to exude pompousness, this one offers a history of gracious cordiality, which we can thankfully still appreciate today.

Warren A. Conrad/Noffsinger Residence

404 FOURTH AVENUE EAST, KALISPELL

THE NAME "CONRAD" BEARS RECOGNITION IN THE FLATHEAD Valley. Along with the Conrad Mansion, Conrad Cemetery and Conrad Drive, the house at 404 Fourth Ave. E. in Kalispell is also part of the family's legacy.

Like any good "rags-to-riches story," brothers Charles and William Conrad left their Virginia home after the Civil War with little more than a silver dollar between them. However, they found success in hauling freight by riverboat and ox-cart wagons through the Montana Territory.

Charles and William later founded the Conrad National Bank of Kalispell, the Kalispell Townsite Company (along with directors of the Great Northern Railway), and other cattle and mining companies. Their founding of Kalispell was imparted with success upon the arrival of the Great Northern Railway, which used the town as a division point along the railroad.

Their younger brother Ashby (Warren Ashby Conrad) followed in their footsteps and success and helped build the family enterprise. For example, in starting the Conrad National Bank, Ashby worked as a cashier. And with the growing success of the bank, he served as a bank director just the same.

In the spring of 1895, Ashby's brother Charles began building upon the plans for his own home (which is now the Conrad Mansion). At the same time, Ashby was busy with plans of his own and married Caroline Green on June 26, 1895. These two events likely urged Ashby to have a mansion for himself, as he was now a married man of considerable position, and without a home to rival his older brother.

However, Ashby spared himself the nuisance of mansion-building and bought a suitable one that had already been built by pioneer rancher and businessman J.L. Cox in 1894. Cox sold his mansion to Ashby, who bought it as a gift for his newlywed wife Caroline in 1896.

Except during the summers, when the house was likely to be found empty as Ashby and Charles had summer cottages on Hawksnest Island on Foys Lake, the mansion must have suited the Conrads well, and for good reason. The house was built with the best of construction with many fine features and appointments of the day.

While the house is predominately of Colonial-Revival style, it has many flourishes of the popular Queen-Anne style as well – a combination of architectural styles that was quite common at the end of the 19th century.

The Centennial Exhibition of 1876 inspired newfound attention to the colonial past of America. It also inspired a return to colonial architecture as in the plain symmetry, two stories and small gabled dormers at the front of the house (think of colonial buildings in Philadelphia or Boston). The use of brick is also obvious, as brick was used in building earlier colonial homes as well, and several purveyors offered locally-fired brick at the time.

The turret at the side of the house – with its pattern-shingles – is an obvious Queen-Anne adornment. As there are few homes with Queen-Anne towers or turrets in the Flathead Valley, this one is worth appreciating for the tower located on the north side of the home.

Other Queen-Anne features include the stained-glass windows and the wrap-around porch, which was carefully reconstructed in 2003 from old photographs with colonial-style columns. The balcony over the bay window at the side of the house is another Queen-Anne feature (as Colonials tend to be plain-sided). The iron fencing along the perimeter of the property, with spearhead finials, is also another touch of history from the Queen-Anne era.

The Conrads resided in the home until Ashby passed away in 1922. Afterward, Caroline rented the home for several years until selling it to its other namesake, George Noffsinger, manager of the Glacier National Park Saddle Horse Company.

Fortunately for history, Noffsinger and later owners have taken great care of the home, allowing us to appreciate this fine Colonial Revival and its history.

Dean Rental Property

19 FIFTH AVENUE EAST, KALISPELL

HISTORIC LANDMARK HOMES COME IN ALL SHAPES, SIZES AND styles. The Dean Rental Property at 19 Fifth Ave. E. in Kalispell proves that even a small house can be a big part of local history.

In fact, this seemingly ho-hum cottage hides its historical significance quite well – a significance that helps explain the mystery of the carriage house that was once part of the Charles Conrad mansion complex.

Some folks may recall, whether from memory or photos, that the Conrad property once had an elaborate barn, carriage house and stable complex. These once stood more or less behind the Conrad mansion along what is now Woodland Avenue, with about another 70 acres of property that is now mostly Woodland Park.

The mansion and carriage house were designed by Kirtland Cutter of Spokane for Charles Conrad and his wife Alicia. Incidentally, Cutter designed the 1893 Chicago World's Fair "Idaho Building" – a favorite among the crowd of some eighteen million visitors. And he eventually designed several hundred buildings in Spokane, including many that are designated historical landmarks.

The fanciful, turreted carriage house, where the Conrad's night watchman once kept guard, seemed to have disappeared sometime after Alicia moved away in 1923 (Charles died in 1902 and was the first person buried in the Conrad Cemetery – reportedly).

Well, the carriage house didn't disappear. And it wasn't hauled off for salvage either. In fact, it didn't go very far at all – part of it is right here.

Indeed, this house is one of the pieces of the former Conrad carriage house. It's transformation, however, requires a bit of explanation.

In 1927, Alonzo J. Dean retired from his long-held position as manager of the J.C. Penney Store in Kalispell. While president of the Kalispell Chamber of Commerce, rather than pass time idly by, Dean traded retirement for real estate investment.

In 1928, Dean seized the opportunity to purchase the Conrad carriage house, barn and stable complex. Perhaps he saw greater opportunity, perceiving that "the parts" were worth more than "the whole," as Dean divided up the massive carriage house into five separate parts which are now four separate houses and one business.

Dean converted and lived in "the turreted" portion of the former carriage house, which sits along Woodland Avenue (and has a wonderful history all its own). And he converted this section of the carriage house into a rental property to generate income.

In converting the pieces of the carriage house into their own unique, separate homes, Dean hired the help of Kalispell architect Fred Brinkman. And for the most part, Brinkman masterfully kept the parts of the original carriage house in tact, finishing them as necessary and adding facades inspired by the popular styles of the day.

With this house, Brinkman adapted the popular Tudor-Revival style. And even on a relatively small scale, the half-timbering on the sides of the front dormer at the steep-gabled roof, an arcade wing, and the arched entryway, are typical hard-to-miss Tudor-revival elements that adorn the house.

And unlike the barn and other parts of the original carriage house, including the oak timbering that were shipped by rail to places beyond Montana, this section didn't go very far at all, and remains quite close to two other sections (on the opposite block along Woodland Avenue) with the other two still remaining nearby.

Fortunately, through years of different occupants and owners, this portion of the carriage house – and a good home in its own right – has been well kept. Much like the historical secret it keeps safely underneath its modesty.

Demersville Cemetery

115 SHEFFORD LANE, KALISPELL

IN THE LATE 1880S, DEMERSVILLE WAS A BUSTLING BOOMTOWN. Today, it seems hardly more than a memory. Demersville was supposed to be Kalispell, but when the Great Northern Railway chose to put a division point at Kalispell, Demersville became obsolete literally overnight.

Gregg Street, Foy Street, and the rest of Demersville had their share of saloons, "gambling hells" and pleasures aplenty, but Demersville had only one of many other things. For example, Demersville was named after one man: Telephose J. DeMers. Demersville had only one mayor: J. E. Clifford (who later served time in the Montana State Penitentiary). And Demersville had but one cemetery, at the west end of town.

Today, much like the town itself, the Demersville Cemetery is all but forgotten for the most part. Yet the cemetery, and the people interred there, mark a profound history – and tell the history of the Flathead Valley itself.

Those with an interest in local history and ancestry should know that The Museum at Central School in Kalispell has a list of the people buried at the Demersville Cemetery. The list tells the names and ages of the deceased and other insightful information, such as their cause of death.

However, reading the list is not for the light hearted, for when you read the names of those who succumbed to some forgotten disease, or those who served in a long-forgotten war, or the names of those who barely lived beyond the age of 11, or 7, or 11 months, things may seem a bit more somber.

Perhaps even more perplexing are the graves that are missing. Not only are gravestones missing, but many graves themselves are missing – and so are important marks in history as well.

For example, missing is the gravestone of James M. Dunn. Dunn was a prospector who left his home and family in Iowa and traveled to Post Falls, Idaho. Having little luck there, Dunn set out to prospect along Flathead Lake. After crossing Dayton Creek with his horse, Dunn was met by a Kootenai named Pascale. Pascale traveled along with Dunn until they reached the south slope of Angel Hill (which is now in Lakeside) sometime in the late summer of 1889.

Varied accounts tell of a disagreement, argument, or a horse trade gone bad. No matter the cause, the outcome was tragic: Pascale shot Dunn, left him for dead, and hid his body under brush on the hill.

The following spring, Dunn's body was discovered and he was ultimately buried in the Demersville Cemetery in 1890, the same year the cemetery was established. But there is no longer any sign of his grave (ironically, Pascale was buried at the St. Ignatius Mission Cemetery, and no signs of his grave exist either). Thus, there is little to mark Dunn's grave and little to remind us of this fateful tragedy.

Likewise, it seems that other graves in the Demersville Cemetery have been "lost" as well, albeit to flooding or forgetting. Not only is the memory of these souls forgotten, but so is their history – an inextricable part of the history of the Flathead Valley and beyond.

For who among us knows the story of Baby Horn, Julia Dalatte, John Cheley, William Lisle Berge, Martha Livingston? And who can recall the lives and memories of the mill and railroad workers, the Chinese, the Greeks, the Italians and other immigrants, and so many others whose graves have been lost or forgotten?

Indeed, the Demersville Cemetery is a landmark and all that is left of the bygone town of Demersville – and each grave is truly a landmark of history all its own.

George Drew Residence

345 FOURTH AVENUE EAST, KALISPELL

THERE'S MORE TO A HOUSE THAN MEETS THE EYE (MUCH LIKE judging a book by its cover). And there's more to the history of a house beyond its namesake. In the case of the "George Drew Residence," it seems to be quite the misnomer.

The home at 345 Fourth Ave. E. in Kalispell was originally built in 1892 – barely a year after the town itself had been platted and founded. As nearly 100 new homes were being built in the fledgling railroad town of Kalispell, German immigrant Louise Sels and her son Ed found the resolve to build this home for themselves as well.

And so, this cross-gabled, Queen Anne home was one of the earliest built in the new town. It should be noted that the home was commissioned by a woman, which was noteworthy considering the times (as women were unable to vote until the Nineteenth Amendment was enacted in August, 1920).

Louise sold the home to her son-in-law, Arthur Burnes, but continued to live in the home with the extended family. In 1902, Burnes sold the home to Josephine Richards and Ella Bell (note again, the home was owned by two women). Josephine and Ella rented the "large front rooms" to gentlemen until 1905, when they sold the house to George E. and Maude B. Drew.

As new owners, George and Maude made two remarkable improvements to the home. First, they likely added the distinctive, horseshoe-shaped front porch. "Front porch homes" were quite popular then. And it was a feature that added depth (and social "status") to the front of the house, and provided a place to enjoy more idle moments.

Second, they removed the partial, wooden planking at the front of the house and installed a brick sidewalk – an improvement that was lauded in local newspapers at the time. A sidewalk may not seem like anything worth mentioning today, but back then, it was a sign of commitment; a mark of permanence. It was a bold improvement in many ways, considering both the history of Kalispell, and the personal lives of the Drews as well.

George and Maude arrived in Kalispell in 1901. They established a dry goods and grocery store, known then as "Drew and MacDonalds." As their business prospered, they purchased the home to raise their family. In 1912, they sold the store, but decided to keep the house and remain in Kalispell.

As fate would have it, Maude would become the longest resident of the home. She lived in the home from 1905, until her passing in 1959, at the age of 89. She outlived her husband George, who she petitioned for divorce in 1926, alleging his desertion (George passed away two years later, in 1928).

Maude kept the home and raised her two children, Albert and Edna there. Yet sadly, Maude had to bear what no mother should: Maude had to tend to the untimely passing of her son Albert, at the home in 1950.

In retrospect, Maude helped establish the business that helped pay for the home. She owned the home – before she even had the right to vote. She made improvements that literally "paved the way" for progress in the town of Kalispell. And she resided in her home, before World War I, until after World War II, enduring hardships and raising her family all the while.

Yet despite such a history, a home first commissioned by a woman, then owned by two women, and kept for more than 54 years by the same woman, bears the namesake of a man: "George Drew" – which in light of the history of the home, seems to be quite a misnomer.

Perhaps someday, this house will be more appropriately regarded as the "Maude Drew Residence" in honor of the woman who lived in the home for more than 54 years (and 30 years longer than her husband).

Driscoll House

513 THIRD STREET EAST, KALISPELL

ECLECTIC. UNUSUAL. UNIQUE.

These terms accurately describe the home at 513 Third St. E. in Kalispell. It's eclectic, as in being designed in the "French Eclectic" style. It's unusual, as for being an architectural style that is relatively uncommon throughout the United States. And it's certainly unique, as a one-of-a-kind home in its neighborhood (if not all of Northwest Montana).

The French Eclectic style was fashionable during the 1920s and 1930s, although some homes were built in the style later on, such as this one, which was built in 1941.

The style likely gained popularity as soldiers returned home after World War I and brought an appreciation (and perhaps a longing) for the various styles of homes found throughout the French countryside.

The original owner, Maurice Driscoll, built the house as a wedding present for his wife, Mary. Maurice worked as a cashier for the First National Bank. And he was the son of Catherine and Michael Driscoll, a lumber pioneer and businessman who arrived in Kalispell in 1899. Maurice was also a member of the Montana Symphony Orchestra and enjoyed playing music – something he did frequently while entertaining guests in the home and at private affairs and public concerts.

Newspaper articles from the late 1920s report that Maurice was featured playing "Mighty Like a Rose," "Me and My Shadow" and other popular songs of the day as part of an instrumental trio on Flathead Broadcasting Association radio programs. And several "Local Society" articles reported how Maurice, Mary and their two daughters entertained family and friends at the home, treating them with music performed by Maurice as well.

In building the home, Maurice commissioned renowned Kalispell architect Fred Brinkman. Brinkman certainly left his mark on Kalispell – and certainly added unique flair to the neighborhood with this one-of-a-kind home as well.

Even at first glance, the house appears unlike any other in Kalispell, especially since it bears three hallmark traits of the French Eclectic style: a steeply pitched hipped-roof, a massive chimney and "through-the-cornice" or "above the roof" windows.

The masonry walls and circular window also add to the stylistic treatment, as does the columned porch with an eave that flares upward. And overall, the home imparts more of a sense of understated grandeur than overstated lavishness that is also part of the French Eclectic style.

But beyond stylistic traits and building characteristics, architecture is perhaps most meaningful when it conveys a sense of a different time and place. Perhaps Maurice built and styled this house for his wife, so she could feel at home in Montana – just as much as in the French countryside. For standing before this house, and absorbing its French Eclectic style, one could perhaps transcend Montana to someplace in the hills of France.

Duncan Samson Block

EAST SECOND STREET, WHITEFISH

THE CITY OF WHITEFISH OWES MUCH OF ITS HISTORY TO ONE particular day: Oct. 4, 1904, when the first Great Northern Railway train pulled into this "commodious and important" division point (which was formerly located at Kalispell).

In many ways, Whitefish was a railroad boomtown. For example, so many trees were felled in such a short time that the moniker "Stumptown" was quite fitting. And like many other railroad towns, a "Townsite Company" managed the selling of plats within the city. And within just a year after the first train rolled through, Whitefish was incorporated.

Whitefish was planned to be the biggest town along the Great Northern in Montana. Although today, the connection between the railroad and some buildings may be difficult to see. Sure, the Cadillac Hotel (where the Great Northern Brewing Company is now located) just a block away from the railyard, had an obvious connection to the railroad. But the Duncan Samson Block – about six blocks away, at East Second Street and Lupfer Avenue – may have a less obvious connection, although a connection nonetheless.

The block bears the name of its founders Ms. Jemima Ann Duncan, and her business partner Mr. Joseph Adelbert Samson.

Jemima moved from Kalispell to Whitefish to likely make a new start with her three children, as she had recently been widowed. And once settled in Whitefish, she must have seen an opportunity in building a rooming house for railroad workers.

Joseph had lived and worked in Pennsylvania, New York, West Virginia and Kentucky before settling in Whitefish in 1907. He quickly pursued a few business interests, and began procuring railroad ties for the Great Northern Railway.

After hearing of Jemima's plans to build a boarding house, Joseph became her business partner. Together, they financed $33,000 for the construction of this building with boarding rooms above, and shop spaces below. And if construction had been delayed a few months, the building might have been named "The Samson Block" as Duncan and Samson married later that year.

Despite its distance from the railroad tracks, the Duncan Samson Block was nonetheless closely serving the Great Northern Railway, as it provided much-needed housing for the railroad workers.

The upper story of the building, in some form or another, was always living spaces – spaces that housed the hardiest of railroad men, and the most sophisticated "urban" transplants, who both mingled in the building's legacy.

The professional spaces below also have some unique legacies of their own. For example, a chiropractor has been in one of the spaces since the 1930s (and one still is). And throughout its history, despite changes in taste and names, one would have always found food of some kind at 307 E. Second Ave., from the former Grist Mill Bakery, the Breadline Deli – or the Swift Creek Cafe, which operates at the location today.

Despite the preservation of much of the original brick exterior, the coal hatches, and many of the original doors and finishings, perhaps the most interesting aspect of the building is the "possum trot" or "breezeway" as it is more commonly known.

As you step through the front door, you step back in time, into a breezeway with windows of the shops and apartments on either side, a feature hardly seen since the early nineteenth century.

Speaking of windows, the building also features an early architectural style perhaps best described as: "put 'em wherever ya need 'em." And since most of the basement windows and other upper-story windows have been filled in with brick, it makes the semblance of the structure even harder to ascertain – but somehow that very quirkiness makes the building seem all the more interesting.

So to appreciate a unique breezeway building with many of its original traits, one with a strong connection to railroading and commerce, and one built in the boomtown era by two Whitefish pioneers, then look no further than the Duncan Samson Block.

Dunsire House

545 SECOND AVENUE EAST, KALISPELL

PEOPLE WHO LIVE IN SMALL HOMES TEND TO HAVE BIG HEARTS. Which explains why there's sometimes a lot more to a "landmark" home than just grandeur or décor. The Dunsire House at 545 Second Ave. E. in Kalispell provides a little perspective on this theory concerning things big and small.

The home was originally owned as a rental property by Isabelle and David Sturtevant. It was built between 1891 and 1894 (the record books aren't too precise and list it as an "Old Style" home, and it was originally built in Demersville and later moved to its current location). Despite its small size, the home features a full front porch with columns, a south-facing bay window, a front-facing dormer, and other stylish appointments of the late Victorian era. And with two bedrooms and one bath, the home offered ample space, without forsaking economy, considering the lifestyle of its earliest occupants.

In 1900, the home would assume its namesake and legacy when Mr. Andrew Dunsire and his wife Isabella purchased it.

Mr. Dunsire was born in Methilhill, Fifeshire, Scotland. Growing up in the coastal town probably helped make it easier for him to immigrate to the Flathead Valley, which he did on May 23, 1888. Dunsire found work as the assistant post master at Ashley (a bygone town, now part of Kalispell) and later as a clerk in a general store.

He then became a purser on the "Crescent" steamboat, which plied the waters of Flathead Lake between Polson and the once-upon-a-time town of Demersville, and points in between. A purser is responsible for two things that seem to fit Dunsire's personality: looking after people; and handling money – as he would do both in one capacity or another throughout his life.

Yet in forging a new life in a new land, Dunsire did not forsake his past. He never forgot his childhood sweetheart, Isabella Ritchie. When she left Bishopmill, Elgin, Elginshire, Scotland and arrived at the train station in Missoula, Dunsire met her there. The reunited couple then went straight to the Episcopal Church and were married there.

The newlywed Dunsires then traveled to Kalispell and settled there – and settled they did as they made this cozy house their home for more than 50 years.

Despite the modest living space, the Dunsires still made room to accommodate Isabella's sister, Agnes Ritchie, Andrew's nephew, and other boarders and guests. The couple was also generous with their time, money, and efforts outside the home, and both Mr. and Mrs. Dunsire participated in many civic-minded organizations.

For example, Mr. Dunsire served as the Flathead County assessor from 1897 through 1904. He also served the Kalispell Volunteer Fire Department, and held the position of secretary in that organization. He was also an accomplished tenorist and sang at many weddings, funerals, church ceremonies and other special affairs.

While forging a legacy of their own, the Dunsire's seemed to have never forgotten their Scottish heritage. Reminders of Scotland would grace their home, and even were used as gifts, such as Scottish heather that somehow found its way into a bride's bouquet, and other gift arrangements made by the subtle hand and thoughtful grace of Mrs. Dunsire on numerous occasions.

After years of marriage, and serving the community, Andrew Dunsire passed away in 1947 – but not before the Dunsires celebrated their 50th wedding anniversary at the home. It was an occasion when the "tiny house" swelled with flowers, telegrams and friends old and new who came to visit the Dunsires – one of the most respected and appreciated couples of their day. Isabella remained in the family home until her passing in 1952, at the age of 93.

In their lifetime, the Dunsires packed this modest home full with a legacy of life and love – one that could hardly fit in a home twice the size.

Elliot House

828 THIRD AVENUE EAST, KALISPELL

THE LANDMARK, HISTORIC HOME AT 828 THIRD AVE. E. IN Kalispell was originally built around 1911 by Hiram Johnson.

Johnson initially came to Montana in 1893 as a homesteader, and soon took up orcharding apples and cherries near Flathead Lake. Johnson was enterprising, his business blossomed, and soon he was selling produce door to door in Kalispell. Johnson later moved to Kalispell with his wife, so their three children could attend public school "in town."

In 1917, the Johnsons sold the home to John and Elizabeth Elliot – for whom the house is named after. Like Johnson, Elliot was an enterprising man. Along with his brothers (William and Tom) he owned and operated the "Elliot Brothers Company" dealing in general merchandise and wholesale groceries.

Sadly, John Elliot passed away in 1919, just two years after moving into the home. The Elliot Brothers enterprise continued to succeed, and eventually operated their "old reliable, one price" stores and held interest in other businesses in Bigfork, Columbia Falls, Creston, Kalispell, Kila, Somers and Whitefish. They also took over businesses such as the Flathead Commercial company and Yegen Brothers (of Billings). And in retrospect, the Elliot Brothers not only endeavored, but defined early mercantile trade in northwest Montana.

Although John passed away, Elizabeth Elliot remained in the home until 1946. She remodeled the home, giving it more of the appearance it has today, including a subtle – or somewhat annoying – design element (depending upon your asymmetry/aggravation threshold).

Overall, the home features obvious symmetrical and geometric patterns and elements that were popular in the early 20th century.

For example, the gabled roof at the front of the house forms the shape of a triangle at the second story. The eave returns at the corners of the roof also create well-balanced, proportioned triangles – unlike many psuedo-historic commercial buildings and "McMansions" that often have eave returns that are way out of balance (or just plain wrong).

And while there's obvious symmetry with the dormers at each side of the house, the window panes and other features, there is perhaps a bit of not-so-subtle asymmetry.

The front of the house was once an open, full-width porch. Elizabeth Elliot had it enclosed in 1927, as many other homeowners in Kalispell were remodeling and doing the same.

As with the rest of the house, there is much symmetry in the porch design: there are four columns flanked by a set of Craftsman-styled windows with symmetrical patterns. However, the front door is slightly off center – or way out of place – depending upon who you ask. And there are four panels of windows on one side of the door – and five on the other side.

For some, asymmetry like an off-centered front door is what makes a home unique. For others, it's enough to make them want to get a saw, level, and hammer and move the door over into its "proper place" at once.

However, reckoning the front door hardly matters considering how the Elliot family legacy is an intrinsic part of Flathead Valley history.

And while the association with the "Elliot Brothers" is part of the heritage of this landmark home, its character was not just defined by who "wore the pants in the family," but by Elizabeth and the Elliot children as well.

Ferguson House

320 FOURTH AVENUE WEST, KALISPELL

AT 320 FOURTH AVE. W., STANDS A FOURSQUARE COTTAGE THAT harks back to the Victorian era with much of its original Queen Anne style.

Today, it's an historical home listed on the National Register of Historic Places. Yet when it was built sometime around 1897, this cottage was a hallmark of the Queen Anne style during its height of popularity.

The home is known as the Ferguson House, named after its builder and first owner, Frederick Ferguson. Ferguson built the home while he worked for the Great Northern Railway – and while William McKinley was the 25th President and the United States was still recovering from the Panic of 1893.

Ferguson lived in the home with his wife Elsie and her son until 1904, when they moved to Whitefish, along with the Great Northern Railroad as it moved its division point from Kalispell to Whitefish as well. While Ferguson lived and worked in Whitefish, he kept this home and rented it. And so the home began its long history as a rental property with tenants such as a Civil War veteran officer, a saloonkeeper, a painter and other notable folks.

And like the grandiose Queen Anne homes of prominent railroad tycoons, lumber barons, and copper kings, this home shares many similarities – although on a much smaller scale.

For example, like many Queen Anne homes and mansions, the home has a prominent front gable, layered eaves and a porch that covers the entire front. It also features other elements typical of the Queen Anne style such as "fishscale" siding, a sunray pediment, front columns with attractive spindle work, and a prominent chimney.

Perhaps Ferguson, an immigrant from England, was familiar with the Queen Anne style, which had already been quite popular in his homeland. Perhaps as a railroad employee, he was inspired by the homes of the railroad tycoons, or the Victorian-style railroad stations of the East. Or perhaps Ferguson was inspired by the stately Queen Anne homes of the prominent businessmen whose lumber, copper and goods were hauled by his employer, the Great Northern Railway.

Yet no matter his inspiration, Ferguson left a legacy with this home, which had been well-maintained and kept in his family until the early 1970s. And fortunately, the home still stands for us to appreciate its Victorian-era style and be reminded of the legacy of bygone times in Kalispell history.

First Presbyterian Church

524 MAIN STREET, KALISPELL

THE UNMISSABLE LANDMARK FIRST PRESBYTERIAN CHURCH, AT 524 Main St. in Kalispell, is part of the Kalispell Courthouse Historic District. While this says little about the notion of "a separation of church and state," it does say a lot about one of Kalispell's unique neighborhoods that was designed around the courthouse – and the church – which were both an integral part of the community.

And no matter your devotion or denomination, appreciating this landmark requires a bit more background of religion and early local history.

Reverend George M. Fisher first came to Montana in 1882. He preached the first sermon in this area of Missoula County in 1886 (which later became Flathead County in 1893). Reverend Fisher also established the first Presbyterian congregation in Kalispell in 1891.

This was a time when Lakeside was known as Chautauqua – a nod to the religious/education revivals held there (the first of which were held in Chautauqua, New York; hence, the name). It was a time when "Kalispel" (yes, it was originally spelled with only one "l") could be heard spoken in Salish "qlispél." And it was a time when "muck" was an endearing way to describe the thoroughfares in the barely laid town site.

It was against this backdrop that Reverend Fisher and his congregation built the first church in Kalispell, which also had the first steeple bell that tolled in the Flathead Valley. That same bell (a model #48 built by the Cincinnati Bell Foundry

Company) no longer hangs in the steeple, but stands in front of the church today. It's a rare piece of local history you can still touch and admire along Main Street.

As Kalispell boomed, so did the need for a larger church. Fortunately, in retrospect, the church did not follow its original plan to rebuild in 1904, but expanded in 1925, along with tremendous community support and a bold new source of inspiration. In the time between 1904 and 1925, railroad tycoon James J. Hill and his Great Northern Railway established and built "an architecturally cohesive" railroad tourist destination nearby: Glacier National Park.

Even before the bill establishing Glacier National Park was passed, Hill implored wealthy, patriotic Americans to visit the "American Alps" and "See America First" and deplored any notion of them going abroad to the Swiss Alps instead.

For Hill, the area of Glacier National Park was truly the "American Alps" and he insisted on all the buildings looking the same based upon his designs, which were inspired by the Swiss Chalet style of the Swiss Alps, but also the Forestry Building at the 1905 Lewis and Clark Centennial Exposition in Portland, Ore.

Hill's Swiss-Chalet-meets-massive-pioneer-log-style used for the buildings in Glacier National Park were the source of inspiration for architect Fred Brinkman, who designed this landmark church (and other homes in a similar Tudor-Revival style in Kalispell).

Brinkman's designs were realized in 1925 with many similarities to the hotels and chalets in Glacier National Park including the log rafters, decorative half-timbering, river rock masonry, clapboard siding, and other elements, better seen than written about.

And perhaps in marking the end of one era, and the beginning of another, Reverend Fisher dedicated this church and center to the community in 1927 – a place that has since provided inspiration, in more ways than one.

Flathead County Courthouse

PHOTO BY LIDO VIZZUTTI

800 S. MAIN STREET, KALISPELL

THE FLATHEAD COUNTY COURTHOUSE BUILDING, AT 800 S. MAIN St. in Kalispell is rather unmissable in more ways than one. A bit of texting-and-driving gone wrong and one could drive straight into it (literally). And as one of the tallest, most formidable buildings in the area, it stands unavoidably to the south, visible from anywhere along Main Street in Kalispell.

It's a unique building with a history borne of necessity. The Flathead Valley was initially part of Missoula County. As more settlers came to the valley in the 1880s and 1890s, trekking to the county seat in Missoula became unbearable. The trip could take a week depending upon the weather, trail conditions, and other factors of traversing a route that was still little more than a cow path at some places.

By 1892, the Great Northern Railway helped establish Kalispell as a town, and also created the need for a closer county seat. After successful legislation, Flathead County was established in 1893. And Kalispell was chosen as the county seat in 1894.

By 1895, the Flathead County government had been created. However, there was no official place of county business, aside from make-shift courts and court offices scattered about Kalispell. After years of make-do county business, local leaders decided something had to be done – Flathead County needed an official place for business.

On June 17, 1902, a site for a new, permanent county courthouse and jail was selected. The Kalispell Townsite Company, directed by Charles E. Conrad, sold about 2.75 acres of land to the county for the courthouse. The land was formerly part of the original 160-acre, homestead patent of John Sell.

Certainly, a county with grand promise needed a grand building. And there was perhaps no finer model of a government building than the Montana State Capitol. So Flathead County officials chose the architectural firm of Charles E. Bell and John H. Kent (Bell & Kent) of Helena – the same architects who designed the Montana State Capitol. Consequently, the Capitol building and the Flathead County Courthouse building share many conceptual similarities (although the building of the Flathead County Courthouse seems to have been spared much of the graft and corruption that was involved in building the Capitol).

Today, the courthouse building may seem like a dreadful bastion of bureaucracy. However, even the most tedious county administration hardly compares to the dread Fred LeBeau faced at the courthouse on April 2, 1909 – when he was executed by hanging at the gallows outside the courthouse, as punishment for his crime of murder.

Also, the building was designed with a clock tower – although a clock has yet to be installed and the history of its whereabouts remains unknown.

These are just a couple of the many "interesting" facts to be found in courthouse history, while in hindsight, the very location of the courthouse – smack in the middle of a busy roadway – remains suspect.

The circular roundabout was established in the 1970s – several decades after the courthouse was built in the early 1900s, when Main Street and Kalispell itself did not extend much further to the south. Besides, back then it was the very intention to have the courthouse anchor the opposite end of the "commercial district," about a half-mile to the south of the railroad depot.

Indeed, the Flathead County Courthouse is a unique building, at a unique location, with a unique history – all deserving of much greater appreciation (beyond any bureaucracy and paperwork that may get in the way).

HENRY GOOD RESIDENCE

820 THIRD AVENUE EAST, KALISPELL

THE LANDMARK AT 820 THIRD AVE. E. IN KALISPELL PROVIDES A good reminder about "what's good for the home, is good for the heart" (and vice versa). It's one of those fun, almost personified homes that always seems to welcome you with a smile.

The home bears the name of Henry Good, a man who played a significant role in making Kalispell what it is today. He was a successful farmer and logging contractor in Northwest Montana. His business operations exemplified success and he also served as a Flathead County commissioner in the early 1900s.

Yet misfortune often seems to ignore success. Tragically, Good suffered the loss of his first wife during the influenza epidemic of 1918, which took a devastating toll on many families in the Flathead Valley. Despite grieving his loss, Good persevered such personal setbacks and tragedies, like many men of his generation.

In 1920, Good married his second wife Alice. Together, the family kept a successful farm just north of Kalispell. Yet they needed a "home in town" during off seasons so they could tend to business matters.

In 1926, they found this home, which was practically new. The original owners, Henry and Lena Nollar built it the year before (the home just switched Henrys when Henry Nollar sold it to Henry Good). The Good family stayed here off and on over the years, and rented the home in between.

Inside, the home featured beautifully crafted "gumwood doors and woodwork" and was graced by Alice's beautiful singing and artistic talents. Alice was an accomplished artist, musician, and teacher, who taught in Kalispell schools before marrying Henry.

And anyone who enjoys a round of golf at the Buffalo Hills Golf Course, should tip their cap to Henry Good. Along with several other golf enthusiasts, Good helped secure funds for the golf course, planned its design, and established its infrastructure. Undoubtedly, Henry conjured some of the ideas for the golf course at home.

As the nation recovered from the Great Depression, a remodeling trend took place in Kalispell. Like many other homes throughout the town, this one was remodeled by local architect Fred Brinkman, some time in the mid-1930s.

Brinkman's remodeling gave the home much of the appearance it has today, which overall, qualifies in the "Colonial Revival" category. However, it's probably best to say the style of the home is more "fun" than anything else, especially since creating a unique style – from a pastiche of styles – was quite popular in the 1930s.

For example, the home features Tuscan columns under a (Greek-Revival) centered portico, (Victorian) eyebrow dormers, (Prairie-style) windows, and a (Bungalow-style) squared frame.

Putting the fun mix of details, colors, and styles aside, passing by to respectfully appreciate this home can be just good fun, particularly if you're having a bad day. For by the time you realize the home is somehow smiling at you – you'll be smiling too.

Goshorn House

820 THIRD AVENUE EAST, KALISPELL

IN A NEIGHBORHOOD FLANKED WITH MANY OTHER HISTORIC homes (some quite fanciful, and colorful), the Goshorn House seems to more humbly anchor the corner at Fourth Avenue East and Fifth Street East in Kalispell.

It is a fine example of a cross-gabled, Queen Anne home. Its decorative shingles, clapboard siding and diamond-shaped windows are all some of the hallmarks of the late Victorian-era. Some of the appointments and finishing on the inside also feature the remarkable craftsmanship of the era as well.

Aside from the exterior and interior features of the home, which are fine examples of the Queen Anne style, the home is not short on history and has its own story to tell – a story that in many ways matters as much as its architecture.

This home was built in 1900 and owned by Robert M. Goshorn – publisher and editor of the Daily Inter Lake newspaper (which was founded in 1889 at Demersville, Montana). Goshorn lived here with his wife Alice, a reporter for the paper, and their children, Joseph and Mildred. Notably, Mildred was in the first class to complete the new four-year course at The Flathead County High School.

The family seemed to enjoy the early years of the 20th-century at the home, however, fate would soon strike a tragic blow. On May 19, 1907, the Goshorns' son Joseph drowned in a canoeing accident on Lake Washington, near Seattle. Reportedly, squalls formed treacherous waves, which swamped and sunk the canoe. Two of Joseph's fellow Stanford University classmates also drowned – and only one of the four young boaters survived.

Such a sorrowful tragedy could devastate any family. Yet in keeping themselves from sorrow and misery, the Goshorns immersed themselves in the business of running the newspaper. And in 1908, they transformed the Inter Lake (a weekly paper) into the Daily Inter Lake (the daily newspaper it is today).

In so doing, the Daily Inter Lake became an enterprise, and came a long way from its first publication on August 10, 1889 as The (Demersville) Inter Lake, which was then a two-page newsprint for a hell-roaring town whose advertisers included stage coach lines, folks who lost guns and grain seeders alike, and proprietors who kept "coffins and caskets on hand" to fill special orders on "short notice."

After establishing the daily paper, Goshorn later sold the Daily Inter Lake in 1913, to a company formed by a group of "progressives." Progressivism was teeming at the time in Kalispell and around the nation due to Theodore Roosevelt's unsuccessful 1912 presidential campaign under his "Progressive Party."

Despite the sale, Alice continued to contribute to the paper. And just a casual glance at the early writings will evidence how she and the paper both shared little hesitation when it came to addressing ornery persons and the controversies of their day (such as milk being served in schools – and other things we hardly think about today).

Before his death in 1937, Goshorn served the U.S. Land Office as a receiver for the Taft administration and a register for the Harding administration.

So the next time you're around the corner of Fourth Avenue East and Fifth Street East, be sure to take a look at the humble house on the corner. While the exterior may seem mild compared with its neighbors, it's a place with an important history, where many early newspaper articles were likely conjured and debated, and a place where one of Kalispell's honorable, early families once lived.

Graham House

825 SIXTH AVENUE EAST, KALISPELL

Even if you're not paying attention, the moment you pass by the house at 825 Sixth Ave. E. in Kalispell, you'll likely take notice. It is the location of the Graham House, which may leave you wondering whether you just traveled back in time – or forward. It's a chic, Art Moderne-style home that is extremely rare in more ways than one.

The house bears the namesake of Wilbur and Celeste Graham, who built the home in 1942, during World War II. It was an unsettling time in America – a time of collective sacrifice that no generation has known since (and perhaps few truly understand today). Goods and provisions were rationed for "the war effort" and building materials were quite scarce. Yet remarkably, this house would become one of the few built in Kalispell during the war.

This was also a time of resourcefulness. Aside from victory gardens, Americans found clever ways to make things last longer. They devised clever substitutes, and re-used, recycled, and otherwise "made do" with whatever they had. In this spirit, Wilbur Graham, a building contractor, likely found the means to assemble the materials to build this unique home.

And while building materials were rare, so too was the style the Grahams chose for their home: the Art Moderne, or "Streamline Moderne" style. Streamline Moderne is much like Art Deco, but without all the ornamentation (it is a sleeker, more "streamlined" version, if you will). Streamline Moderne was a style that looked to the future with frugality in mind.

In nearly every way, this house is a textbook example of the Streamline Moderne style, and has nearly all of the hallmarks of the style, including gentle curves (instead of sharp corners); a preference for horizontal orientation accentuated by a flat roof; smooth surfaces (especially stucco); and a light-colored exterior (whites and natural colors were preferred, although the original color of the home was rather pinkish).

Streamline Moderne also took cues from industrial and transportation designs of the late 1930s. Here, the "porthole" at the front door is a nod to the nautical elements of ships, which were an important feature of the style as well.

What also makes the Graham House unique (aside from being one of the few examples of the style in Montana), is that it is a residence – most of the dabbling in Art Moderne involved commercial buildings. Incidentally, Wilbur built the long garage at the back of the property so he could work in his office there, and again honored the Streamline Moderne style by making the garage/office an elongated, horizontal structure that matched the house.

And while Wilbur passed away in 1958, Celeste lived in the home for nearly 60 years, until she passed in 2001 (a truly remarkable time for any house to be cared for by an original owner).

The Graham House should be appreciated for its style and form, and as one of the rare examples of Streamline Moderne in Montana. It should nonetheless be appreciated as a symbol: it is a house that embodies a rare blend of ingenuity, resourcefulness and optimism that seldom finds its way to the drawing board.

And perhaps more importantly, the home should be appreciated as a unique landmark – built in the rarest of progressive styles, during the worst of trying times, and in a defining manner of American spirit.

GRANT/CLIFFORD HOUSE

126 FOURTH STREET EAST, KALISPELL

IN 1898, CARPENTER WARREN J. LAMB BUILT A TWO-STORY HOME at 126 Fourth St. E. While Lamb's handiwork was part of several early homes that were built in Kalispell, this one perhaps best showcases the ideals of the era and the various architectural styles that were popular in the day.

The home was built around the time the Spanish-American War broke out. Annie Oakley was clamoring for women's rights and espousing how women were also virtuous as sharpshooters and soldiers. John D. Rockefeller and his Standard Oil Company owned more than 80 percent of America's oil, and citizens were developing a more positive outlook as the United States began to recover from the economic turmoil of the Panic of 1893.

On the outside, the house is an interesting mix of popular styles from the late 19th century. Prairie, Craftsman and Arts and Crafts styles were combined in a unique mix that we can fortunately still appreciate today.

The home takes part of its name from James. J. Grant, who purchased the home in 1907. Grant lived in the home with his wife Mary and their five children – the house was home to seven people who all lived together and without many of our modern-day conveniences.

Grant was an Irish immigrant who served in the American Civil War. He was noted as a scout for cavalry commander

General George Armstrong Custer. After the Civil War, Grant continued his service-minded pursuits. He put aside his mining and farming work, and served as a game warden, deputy sheriff and deputy U.S. Marshall.

In 1926, the other part of the home's namesake took ownership. Cecil Clifford and his wife Margaret lived in the home until 1953. Both Cecil and Margaret were ordained Methodist ministers. And Cecil went on to become a doctor and director of religious education.

The Cliffords may also be responsible for giving the home its third – although less famous – moniker. In the late 1920s, their son left to attend college. During this time, they corresponded by writing letters (telegraphs were fading out of fashion and long-distance telephoning was unreliable, if not financially unpleasant). As their son pined for home in their correspondence, the home took on the name "Homomyne" (a play on words for "home of mine"). "Homomyne" stuck and was taken up by relatives, friends and neighbors at the time.

Today, the home still retains many of its turn-of-the-last-century charms. It's hard to miss the low-hipped roof with exposed rafters and wide eaves, which hark to an eclectic mix of Prairie and Arts and Crafts styles that were popular in the 1890s. The mixed use of geometric lines and patterns are also a nod to these styles and hallmarks of the Craftsman style as well.

As a carpenter, Lamb also made interesting appointments on the interior as well. For example, built-in shelves parsed the living room and dining rooms. Lamb also crafted wood paneling for the walls along the stairway. And the red and green exterior colors reflect the original red and green light fixtures and wall sconces that were installed inside the home.

While the echoes of five children playing about, and the pinings for "Homomyne" may seem unobvious today, they can remind us how every home has stories to tell.

Green/Bjorneby House

312 SIXTH AVENUE EAST, KALISPELL

KALISPELL WAS ORIGINALLY A RAILROAD TOWN. AND LIKE MANY homes in Kalispell, the home at 312 Sixth Ave. E. shares a history with the railroad – a very close history.

The building of the home began in 1891, the time when Kalispell briefly became known as "Harrington" when the postmaster named the town after himself (Kalispell became the official name of the town on Jan. 2, 1892).

The home was built by Wesley B. Green, who later became the superintendent of the Kalispell Division for the Great Northern Railway. In June of 1892, the Great Northern announced plans to build a passenger depot in Kalispell using "the finest brick that can be obtained."

As the railroad division boss, Green was in charge of building the railroad depot (incidentally at the same time he was building his own home).

At the time the railroad depot was being built, Kalispell was rather open and sparse. Yet there must have been plenty of places where "the obvious" could hide. For if somebody had seen the obvious, they would have noticed that Green's house was being made of the same "finest brick that can be obtained" as the railroad depot.

Indeed, while supervising the construction of the railroad depot, Green actually stole enough bricks from the railroad depot to build his own home – and nobody made the connection until quite some time later, or at least, didn't have much to say about it.

Kalispell was then "home of a horde of trainmen and trackmen" and Green was their boss. So if anyone figured out that Green was using the bricks for his house instead of the railroad depot, they had plenty of incentive to keep mum.

However, railroad officials eventually discovered Green's brick diversion scheme. Green was dismissed, and since the home was made with bricks that belonged to the Great Northern Railway, Great Northern officials put a lien on the home.

Ironically, a photo of the home was published in the "Great Northern Country," a travel guide published in 1895 by the Great Northern Railroad. It included a photo of the W.B. Green Residence and boasted of its substantial brick structure. The photo also showed a horse-and-buggy in front – and practically nothing else surrounding the home (which looked like a farmhouse on an open field).

Later, during the early 1900s, the home was owned by John Moore, the founder of the Flathead Herald-Journal newspaper. Moore later sold the home to its other namesake, the Bjorneby family.

George and Elida (née Retveit) Bjorneby lived in the home from 1916 to 1926. George Olaus Bjorneby, and his brother Emil, were proprietors of the Bjorneby Brothers Milling Company and were well-respected, reputable businessmen of their day. Incidentally, George Bjorneby was granted U.S. Patent No. 1280377 for an "Improvement in Shock-Absorbers," which issued in 1918. Undoubtedly, Bjorneby worked on this patent while at the home.

The house was later owned by Iver and Florence Hanson (1926-1936). The Hansons sold the home to high school principal Titus Kurtichanov. In the 1940s, Kurtichanov hired architect Fred Brinkman to remodel this out-dated "product of the gay nineties" into a Tudor-style home, which was far more fashionable at the time.

Brinkman removed the grand entrance and original wrap-around porch, but added a garage and a small addition to the home. Today however, the home looks a little more like its original Victoria, Queen-Anne style.

The typical Tudor-style half-timbering that Brinkman added has been removed and the stucco siding has disappeared. And the asymmetrical roof line and stained-glass transom are still intact and provide hints of the original appearance of the home – a home that has much in common with the Great Northern Railway, much like the history of Kalispell itself.

HOUSTON/PARKER HOUSE

604 THIRD AVENUE EAST, KALISPELL

THE HOUSE AT 604 THIRD AVE. E. IN KALISPELL MAY APPEAR SOMEwhat unassuming nowadays. But it has a bold history and marks a time when the steamboat ceded to the railroad, and Demersville ceded to Kalispell as the "Queen City" of northwest Montana.

Like some of its early residents, the house on Third Avenue East wasn't originally from Kalispell – it was built in Demersville and later moved to Kalispell.

The 19th-century boomtown of Demersville was a popular steamboat port serving the north end of Flathead Lake. The area was originally known as "Gregg's Landing" and later took its name from Telesphore Jacques DeMers, a native of Montreal who helped develop the area.

With all of its progress, most residents assumed that the Great Northern Railway would certainly establish a division point at Demersville. However, railroad officials instead chose Kalispell.

Ironically, Demersville boomed with the popularity of one form of transportation (steamboats) – and met its fate with the advent of another (railroads). And when the Great Northern declared that Kalispell would be the new division point, people left Demersville for Kalispell almost overnight, taking their possessions, livestock and in some cases, even their homes with them.

According to property records, the home at 604 Third Ave. E. was moved about four miles from Demersville to Kalispell in 1909.

In 1910, Dr. William Taylor purchased the relocated home. Dr. Taylor served local patients and was also a surgeon and county coroner. He held his practice until 1914 when yet another interesting trade involving the home took place. This time, the house didn't change location – just doctors.

That is, Dr. Taylor swapped houses and medical practices with Dr. Hugh Houston, who practiced in Whitefish. Much like the house itself, Dr. Houston made a new start in Kalispell (several months before he moved into the home, his wife died from trauma suffered in a tragic hunting accident).

Dr. Houston set up his medical practice in a bedroom downstairs and lived in the house with his three daughters and later, his second wife. Needing more space, the family added the kitchen, dining room and porch.

The Houstons sold the home in 1927 to William Parker, who bought it as a Christmas present for his wife, Mable. Parker was in the business of developing refineries and had traveled extensively. Nonetheless, the home remained in the Parker family and was passed down to Parker's daughter and later his granddaughter.

The unique appearance of the house, and its mark of a vintage era, is perhaps mostly due to the mirror-image gabled dormers above the full front porch, which has balusters and columns that frame the front entrance. The porch may appear modest nowadays, but it marks a time long since past when a front porch stylishly let residents be closer to nature and their neighbors.

While the back porch and carport are certainly 20th-century additions, some less-than-obvious traits of its original era are still intact. As the Victorian era gave way to later architectural styles, symmetry and geometry played an important role in defining both the structure and appearance of a home.

At the side of the house, for example, the deliberate, pyramid layout of the windows is obvious. The three windows on the first floor mirror the broad base of the foundation. The two windows on the second floor mark the corners of the roof eaves. And the one window in the attic marks the peak of the gabled roof.

And while the home may have assumed a more humble stance today, it's nonetheless a bold reminder of local history.

Iseminger/Graham House

611 SECOND AVENUE EAST, KALISPELL

"STYLE" AND "CATEGORY" ARE NOT FRIENDS. THE FORMER TRIES to outdo the latter – while the latter tries to keep the status quo. Despite their occasional agreement, theirs is a tumultuous relationship, one that often yields confusion.

And so it is for the Iseminger/Graham House at 611 Second Ave. E. in Kalispell. At first, the home seems to fit quite nicely into the category of "Craftsman" or "Bungalow." However, the house is more representative of the "Colonial Revival Style" (so much for style and category pretending to get along).

The 1877 Philadelphia Centennial is often cited as the inspiration for a renewed interest in American Colonial architecture. And by the early 20th-century, when this home was built, the style was becoming popular – along with a growing sense of nationalistic pride.

Some of the hallmarks of the Colonial Revival style found on the exterior of the home include simple architectural lines; a strict sense of symmetry; and plain details, such as unsophisticated clapboard siding. Other stylistic elements found here include a centered entrance, a porch with classical columns, and modest, dentil trim under the roof eaves.

In 1908, Halbert and Marilla Iseminger sold their rural farm, moved into town and purchased this home, which was an attractive example of a popular and proud style. Soon the extended Iseminger family had resided at the home, including Halbert Jr., who became the listed owner of the home in 1909.

Incidentally, the Isemingers' owned The Men's Fashion Shop in Kalispell, a place where style and category mattered more perhaps than elsewhere. The Isemingers were clever advertisers, and often used intriguing tactics for their advertisements.

For example, one of their ads, in explaining their offerings and service, used various type settings and sizes to make one thing look like another: to wit, "it might seem to you that a MAD-MAN had been plunging on the clothing market ... generous sized BITES have been made off the regular prices... we believe in conservation. So do Messrs. TAFT WILSON and ROOSEVELT."

Despite appearances, at first glance, a "mad-man" did not "bite" former presidents "Taft, Wilson, and Roosevelt" – although one thing was made to look like another for the sake of fashion and style.

Several members of the Iseminger family helped run the business, and also lived in the home for several years. In 1923, the Isemingers sold the home to John and Elsie Graham. The style of the home, with its nationalistic tendencies, likely had a particular appeal to John, who was a US Navy veteran of WWI.

John operated a furniture and appliance store while the Grahams raised their son in the home. Both the elder Grahams remained in the home until their passing: Elsie passed away in 1955, and John remained in the home until he passed away in 1967, leaving behind a legacy of more than 44 years in the same residence.

In contrast to the architecture of the house, Graham's legacy fits neatly into the categories of "thrift" and "well-kept" – which we can all appreciate, especially when it comes to the preservation of a landmark, historic home.

Izaak Walton Inn

290 IZAAK WALTON INN ROAD, ESSEX

THE IZAAK WALTON INN IS STEEPED IN RAILROAD HISTORY. SURE, it's located alongside the railroad tracks, across from the Amtrak station and offers accommodations in luxuriously re-furbished railroad cars (to the dream of rail enthusiasts) – but there are greater connections.

In the early 1900s, James J. Hill, owner of the Great Northern Railway, and his son Louis Hill, began developing Glacier National Park as a tourist destination along the rail line. Louis marketed the park as the "Little Switzerland of America" since the landscape was reminiscent of the Swiss Alps. Hill's exclusive use of Tudor-revival architectural style for the lodges and chalets he developed in the park inspired the connection further.

In January, 1926, the Great Northern Railway changed the name of the Essex station to "Walton" because it was discovered that "fish abound near the station."

The name "Walton" is a nod to the 17th-century, English author Izaak Walton, who wrote "The Compleat Angler" in 1653 and is considered the "patron saint of fishermen." It was not uncommon for fishermen to consider themselves "disciples of Izaak Walton" or belong to the Izaak Walton League of America, one of the nation's first nature conservation organizations.

On June 13, 1939, the Great Northern Railway announced its plans for a "30 room hostelry at Walton." The hotel was to "be of Swiss architectural style to conform with Glacier National

Park structures." And since the lodge was located at "Walton" in honor of Izaak Walton, the name "Izaak Walton Lodge" made sense (although today it's called the Izaak Walton Inn; and the "Walton" station is now known as Essex once again).

The lodge was originally built and leased by the Addison-Miller Company of St. Paul, Minn. The "new $40,000 hotel" formally opened on Nov. 15, 1939. It was designed to accommodate railroad personnel – and the anticipated troves of tourists passing through a new planned entrance to Glacier National Park (although, that plan never came to fruition).

The lodge was proclaimed to be "modern in every detail." The ground floor was designed with a "good-sized lobby, fireplace, newsstand, kitchen and dining room and four master bedrooms with private bath." The second floor had "sixteen spacious rooms with ample baths, closet and locker space," while the third floor was allocated for sleeping quarters for the hotel staff.

The lodge stands alongside a rail yard that was (and still is) critical to railroad operations. Railroad workers toiled on snow removal gangs and locomotive helper-engines, which were added to help eastbound trains make it over the Continental Divide at Marias Pass, with its peak elevation at 5,216 feet. Likewise, helper-engines were taken off westbound trains after they came down the pass.

Incidentally, the Izaak Walton Lodge had nothing to do with Izaak Walton's cottage built centuries before in England, yet they share many peculiarities.

For example, the Izaak Walton Lodge was designed in Tudor-revival style. Coincidentally, the cottage in England was built in the original, 16th-century Tudor style.

The Izaak Walton Lodge was built alongside a railroad. And coincidentally, a railroad was built through the property and alongside the cottage in England (that also had a national forest nearby).

And, the Izaak Walton Lodge was built where a previous "hotel and beanery" (restaurant) once stood – until both were destroyed by fire in 1935. And coincidentally (if not just eerily) the cottage in England caught fire in 1927 and in 1938 from sparks from coal-fired, steam locomotives.

So, if you've never been to the Izaak Walton Inn, or haven't visited in awhile, consider (re-)experiencing it – with its rich history, connections, and coincidences in mind.

Johnson/Benkelman House

1401 SEVENTH STREET EAST, POLSON

IN 1898, THE AREA OF THE FLATHEAD INDIAN RESERVATION known as "Lambert's Landing" became known as "Polson" after the new post office was named after David Polson, a prominent rancher in the area.

Back then, the area was little more than a post office, stage-coach stop and a port of call for steamships. Only about 200 people lived in the area – yet one of them chose to build a stately home at 1401 Seventh St. E., which has long since been a local landmark.

The home was built by John Adolf Johnson (1874-1960), better known as J.A. Johnson, in the common practice of spelling names at the time. Johnson was a prominent man-about-town and a director of the local chamber of commerce. He was a partner in the Security State Bank, which opened on March 26, 1910 – just ten days before the city of Polson was incorporated. Johnson's attendance at civic meetings and social events, including "bridge whilst dinner," was often noted in newspapers throughout his day.

Aside from society and business, Johnson left his mark on the home and grounds. While helping to develop the area, he helped distribute cherry and other orchard trees to ranchers throughout the county (which was a novel idea at the time). His appreciation of trees may account for the chestnut, elm and maple trees on the property, which once extended along a road that has since been abandoned for irrigation Canal B (first surveyed in 1908).

In 1954, Johnson sold the home and property for $18,000 to Ward Benkelman, a prominent physician in the area. Benkelman lived there with his wife Mary and their children. Their son Guy Benkelman recalled how his younger brother Cody was actually named after the wallpaper inside the home.

Guy explained, "we three older boys, Clay, Barney, and I, got to name our younger brother. We were trying to think of a name, staring at the walls in the room upstairs. The wallpaper had a western motif with Wild Bill Cody on it and that's how he got his name – after the Wild Bill Cody wallpaper on our walls."

Guy also spoke about the "mystery" of the first garage that once stood on the property. Guy recalled how his father was smoking salmon in the garage and how "after smoking the fish for so many days, the heat just melted that little 'Chief Smoker' – which went up in flames and took the rest of the place with it."

Mysteriously, the fire department just stood around with his dad and watched it burn and the garage was later rebuilt. The garage and the house stayed in the Benkelman family until 1982.

As for the home itself, overall, its architectural style is a mix of Greek Revival, Craftsman and other genuine Victorian-era appointments.

Inside, many original and early details remain, including the "leaded glass" and ornate American Radiator Co. steam radiators that were likely installed in the 1910s. Although no longer fired by coal, the radiators are a striking reminder of technology from more than a century ago – and the forgotten skill of knowing how to "bleed" a radiator with a "radiator key."

On the outside, the columns at the front of the home invoke the Greek Revival style (even though they are fashioned more in the Craftsman style) – and reveal some of the ideals of the era.

For example, the home was built during the Gilded Age. It was a time when a home was considered a sanctuary, a place to seek refuge from the trivialities of the populace and tribulations of society. So while the columns were meant to be attractive – they also provided a buffer to help shield the home from the outside world as well.

The Johnson/Benkelman House is fine example of popular, late Victorian-era styles and appointments – and a good reminder of how columns, fruit trees, and even wallpaper can have a history all their own.

Madison S. Love Residence

535 THIRD AVENUE EAST, KALISPELL

AT FIRST BLUSH, A STORY ABOUT THE "LOVE RESIDENCE" MAY seem to welcome its share of clichés. But there is a bit more to the story – and this house – than meets the eye.

The residence at 535 Third Ave. E. in Kalispell may seem "odd" at first sight – and that was the very point of its design. The house is a fine example of Shingle-style architecture, which is common along the Eastern coast, where the well-to-do spent their summers, yet somewhat rare in the Northwest.

The Shingle style was an off-shoot of late Victorian ideals and aimed to be big and bold, yet disguise mass and form with surface. It was a style very much concerned with opposition and contrast, yet manifesting overall semblance. And as philosophically challenging as that sounds, so too is perhaps embracing a hallmark of the style: asymmetry – features of the house that seem "off kilter" (yet that were completed with much purpose).

For example, the massive front gambrel roof tends to hide the details of the front porch below, or the contrast between the sharp, recessed roof eaves and the arched, Palladian window. And somehow in the overall impression of the home, "form" tends to conceal "detail" – much how "time" tends to conceal the "history" of the house as well.

The residence was the home of Madison "Matt" S. Love and his wife Alice (née White). They arrived in Kalispell in 1899, at a time when many other Midwesterners found themselves seduced by the bright promise of "the West." The Loves moved into the home in 1909.

The Loves seemed to be a good match – despite a few contrasts (much like their house). For example, Alice was fair-skinned, and fair-handed. She was a talented artist, who for years painted fine porcelains and china (and known to prim herself with a proper lady's touch of embroidery and lace).

In contrast, Matt had rather large, rough hands, the proof of hard work from pulling up his work pants and suspenders, and twisting a pipe wrench (as much as clutching a cigar). Matt was a plumber for many years and only stopped working – at the age of 74 – when his wife Alice sadly passed in 1940.

Together, the Loves helped others learn more than a lesson or two. Like other homeowners during the Great Depression era, the Loves proved that survival and sacrifice somehow shared similar meaning. The Loves lived together in their converted garage and rented out their home to survive and make ends meet.

The Loves also helped others learn, as they often rented the home to school teachers, such as Mrs. (Lucretia) Davis and Mr. (Ertel) Shotwell, who likely planned a lesson or two in their respective apartments inside the house.

The Loves continued to rent the home until 1940 when they both passed away. Alice was buried on Feb. 14, 1940 (yes, a woman named "Alice Love" was buried on Valentine's Day in Kalispell). Several months later, Matt unfortunately passed as well – at the age of 74 (yes, 74 years ago, a man named "Love" died at the age of 74, seven months after his wife).

And sometimes in life, as in art (architecture), there are odd contrasts and coincidences – things that defy proper explanation or expression of understanding – that somehow "make sense" and deserve our whole-hearted appreciation.

LUNDBERG HOUSE

504 FOURTH AVENUE EAST, KALISPELL

APPRECIATING ART AND ARCHITECTURE REQUIRES PERSPECTIVE. Sometimes, it helps to take a step back (literally and figuratively). And in many ways, the landmark house at 504 Fourth Ave. E. in Kalispell can be better appreciated by stepping back in time, some 120 years.

As the 1890s emerged, Kalispell was hardly an idea, while the now-almost-forgotten town of Demersville – the burgeoning metropolis of Northwest Montana – could tout a racetrack for both sport and wager. Demersville could also boast nearly 100 saloons for nearly 1,000 residents, and could easily flaunt her importance as a key navigation point along the Flathead River.

Yet Demersville was just that: an already established place. Its populace was its problem. In contrast, the land that would become Kalispell was little more than a handful of land grants and cattle pasture in the early 1890s.

So for railroad magnate James J. Hill and his cronies (including Charles E. Conrad, the namesake of the Conrad Mansion), establishing a division point along the Great Northern Railway at an existing town meant more competition with existing landowners and less profit. In contrast, establishing a division point at a new town meant no competition and much greater potential for profit.

Thus, Demersville and Columbia Falls were overlooked and the Kalispel Townsite Company8 was established. And

Charles Conrad was appointed to oversee development of the town (and the profits thereof).

Kalispell was formed amid the optimism and caution of the early 1890s. And John Lundberg seemed to have regarded both. He purchased one of the first city lots offered by the Kalispell Townsite Company and also built one of the first brick homes in Kalispell (if not the first brick home).

Sure, Lundberg was a bricklayer – and a bricklayer would likely build a brick house. But a brick house bespeaks commitment. It cannot be moved as easily as a wooden-frame house – like the ones that were literally rolled on logs to Kalispell as people deserted Demersville in droves, taking their houses with them. Incidentally, some unlucky folks saw things the other way around, and moved their houses from Kalispell to Demersville (only to woefully move them back again several months later after Kalispell was chosen as a new, important railroad division point).

Lundberg likely saw great opportunity to build an attractive, brick rental house as people were flocking to Kalispell at the time. Yet Lundberg also seemed practical, or at least practical-minded enough to heed caution, as the design of the house reveals.

Brick is quite permanent – and also quite fireproof. Lundberg seemed keen on building a home to last – and withstand a fire, which was quite a danger back then. The location of the kitchen (at the back of the house, in a separate structure under its own roof) reveals Lundberg's likely aversion to fire and risk. If the kitchen caught fire, the main part of the house could likely be spared by the time the fire brigade arrived.

In taking a step back, Lundberg's optimism and precaution seem to have prevailed. The bricks he laid have served as a home for many tenants and owners over the years. And while their occupations may seem like things of the past – saloon-keeper (George Hodgson), watchman (Clarence Fairbanks) and dairy owner (Earl Hilton) – the brick house they once called home still remains (and offers an altogether different perspective of "progress").

Dr. Alexander D. MacDonald Residence

140 FOURTH AVENUE EAST, KALISPELL

OFTENTIMES, A LANDMARK IS A "LANDMARK" BECAUSE OF ITS location, its history, or maybe its character. Less frequently, a "landmark" is a landmark because of all three, such as the Dr. Alexander D. MacDonald residence on the corner at 140 Fourth Ave. E. in Kalispell.

Sure, any "nice home" behind an attractive cast iron fence can lend charm to a neighborhood. However, there is much more to this home than an ideal or idyll location.

In 1891, Dr. A. D. MacDonald left his Canadian homeland to establish a medical practice in Kalispell (the same year the city itself was established). It was an era of unbounded optimism and unstoppable progress. It was almost a new century, which perhaps explains why the MacDonald family decided to replace their older home that once stood on the property with this one, as if to embrace a new century with a new home, in a new style.

The home was built in 1901 – the same year Vice President Theodore Roosevelt proclaimed, "speak softly and carry a big stick" – and President McKinley was assassinated. The same year the first public telephone debuted in Paris. And the same year that New York became the first state to require license plates on automobiles.

After ten years of building his medical practice, Dr. MacDonald was quite pioneering and prominent, and continued in both regards. He became chief of a private hospital, a Montana state legislator, and a city and county health officer.

Dr. MacDonald also helped lead and establish the Montana State Tuberculosis Sanitarium, noteworthy for its treatment which included a regimen of plentiful clean, fresh air at high altitude – and keeping patients outside regardless of how hot or cold it was outside. In fact, the sanitarium only allowed patients indoors to dress and shelter severe storms.

Mr. and Mrs. MacDonald, were both widely civic-minded. And it should be of little wonder that in pursuing their accomplishments, they used the home to entertain their ambitions as well as their guests, whether friends, family, Masons or members of other organizations.

Undoubtedly, the charming character of the home, both inside and out, lent itself well to any occasion or consideration. Many appointments help create such charm, such as the lead-glass windows, Tuscan-columned porch, ski-style shutters, the bay window, etc.

Overall, if the house must conform to a particular architectural style, the "Shingle style" seems most befitting (with all due exemptions and explanations).

The Shingle style prominently features shingle cladding (obviously), a more "colonial" air (hinted here with the center-hall chimney), and appointments that shun the ostentatious over-doings of the Queen Anne style – as "less" was becoming more vogue than "more."

The incorporation of Shingle-style elements on such a relatively small scale also makes this home unique. Many archetypal shingle style homes are behemoths, yet this smaller home has an illusionary sense of mass and flow.

For example, architects Forrey and Jones placed tiny oval, ornamental windows inside the gambrel-shaped gable, to make it seem bigger than it really is. And by putting a smaller, roof dormer next to it, the gable seems even larger still. And with a landslide of a long, sloped roof – above an open porch – Forrey and Jones made another unique architectural statement about mass and flow as a home built to be "a model of convenience and an ornament to the city."

Yet while the "conveniences" of 1901 hardly rival the modern conveniences of today, this home remains an "ornament" of the city – a unique landmark of place, history and character.

McAllester House

619 SECOND AVENUE WEST, KALISPELL

IN THE EARLY 1900S, KALISPELL WAS STILL QUITE RURAL. DESPITE being a railroad division point, and a center for the agriculture and timber industries, there were still plenty of wide open spaces.

The home at 619 Second Ave. W. proves the point, as it was the only house on the block when it was built in 1909. And its well-preserved farmhouse-style architecture certainly fits, as the home was once surrounded by little more than open fields and nearby horse stables.

The house was built on speculation and hope (much like Kalispell itself). Fellow carpenters Hiram Seeley and William Kelsey believed that Kalispell would continue to grow – and that the home would soon become more valuable as the town progressed. Seeley and Kelsey took their chances, and after framing and roofing the exterior, they lived in the home a few seasons as they finished the interior.

Seeley and Kelsey finished the home and then sold it to James Coleman – a man who, at best, had a troubled time in Montana. Coleman could afford the home with earnings from his proprietorship of a hotel saloon and the Pastime Bar, which he successfully owned and operated during the 1910s.

While few were known to chide Coleman's bartending skills, the Women's Christian Temperance Union (a group determined to rid the nation of drinking and its ills and evils) certainly found a way to put a stop to Coleman's success.

The Temperance Union made life quite difficult for Coleman. Even worse, Coleman's saloon stood across from the YMCA. Thus, the Temperance Union fiercely petitioned against Coleman and his saloon.

Subsequently, Coleman was arrested – not just once – but nearly every day he was at the saloon. Fortunately, a judge finally ruled that despite any temptations that Coleman may or may not have purveyed, he had a right to operate his saloon, despite its seemingly improper location.

However, Coleman's peace was temporary as Prohibition would soon take effect in 1918, coincidentally, about the same time Coleman left the home and Montana.

In 1923, the home was sold to its namesakes: Bradley and Ella McAllester. Mrs. McAllester frequently used the home to entertain friends and family, and host civic groups, including the Past Noble Grand Circle of the (Masonic) Rebekah Lodge, and the Civic Department of the Century Club.

Aside from his longtime position as the manager of the Equity Supply Company, Mr. McAllester was also quite involved with civic organizations. He was a director for the Flathead Game Protective Association. However, Mr. McAllester seemed most devoted to serving farmers in the Flathead Valley. He worked tirelessly as an advocate for local farmers and was a strong supporter of farming causes.

And while the McAllester family seemed to enjoy the home, they perhaps also had to endure a rather difficult time as well.

For carpenters Seeley and Kelsey, the home was a place to hang a hammer, and gain a small advance for their future plans. For Coleman, the home was likely a refuge from the woes of bartending at a time that found Temperance gaining and Prohibition looming.

Yet, unlike the other owners before them, the McAllesters had to watch as their rural, farm-like surroundings were plowed under by real estate development. In 1927, the McAllesters watched as new homes were built on the block. And within several years, the wide pastures just beyond their front door would become sidewalks, alleys and fenced yards – signs that Kalispell would no longer be as rural as it once was.

McGovern/Karcher House

546 SECOND AVENUE EAST, KALISPELL

CORNER HOUSES, BY THEIR VERY LOCATION, OFTEN SERVE A greater purpose far beyond "house and home." They serve as landmarks for those guided by "take a right turn at the brown house on the corner" or "we're the driveway just after the house on the corner" and other means of direction and navigation.

But a house on a corner – with a tower – is going to serve as a landmark whether it wants to or not, as if references to it were part of some predetermined "geographical destiny." Even in a world of GPS and "Google maps," it's hard to trump good, old-fashioned directions such as "turn right at house with a tower on the corner … you can't miss it."

Surely, a Queen-Anne home with a tower on a corner lot is going to be hard to miss. Yet, while the McGovern/Karcher House at 546 Second Ave. E. in Kalispell may be an obvious wayfaring beacon in the neighborhood, the unique history of the home is less obvious.

The home was originally built between 1899 and 1903 by Thomas McGovern. McGovern was an Irish immigrant and a director of the Conrad National Bank of Kalispell. McGovern built several rental homes in the area, and built this fine home for his own family residence.

Aside from the obvious, nearly three-story tower at the south-east corner, the home also has many features typical of the Queen-Anne style. The patterned shingle roof and shingle siding are hallmarks of the era, as are the mansard roof and porch of the rear wing (added on in the early 1900s).

A little less obvious may be the way of life that once transpired here. The McGoverns had seven children. In addition to seven children and two adult parents, the house was home to even more people, as the McGoverns still managed to find room to take in boarders.

"Boarders" were people who paid for a room and were provided with regular meals and lodging. The term "board" refers to the manner in which meals were once served – on a board. And offering "room and board" was a way to offset the costs of keeping the home.

Aside from the cost of building a grand home, the costs of maintaining and heating a home were considerable, and sometimes even beyond the means of what more affluent could afford. Renting rooms was also a way for many to have a sense of company and liveliness about the home.

Mrs. McGovern unfortunately passed in 1903. Mr. McGovern and the children remained there for a few years afterward. In 1907, Mary Karcher purchased the home. Karcher continued letting rooms and taking in boarders of all walks of life within the home.

One of Karcher's longtime boarders, and perhaps best-known in local history, was Chester Brintnall, who boarded here from 1907 until 1925. Brintnall worked for the postal service and helped establish mail delivery service for rural delivery routes. He also served as assistant postmaster, Flathead County commissioner and secretary of the board of Civil Service examiners.

After Karcher's ownership, the home was converted to several apartments, adding even more residents to the list of folks who called "the corner house with the tower" home.

More recently, the home has been converted back to a single-family residence. And while we may never know the history of everyone who lived and boarded here, we can fortunately still appreciate the home as a relic of the Queen-Anne era, and one of the few homes in the Flathead Valley with a tower.

McIntosh House

511 FOURTH AVENUE EAST, KALISPELL

THE HOUSE AT 511 FOURTH AVE. E. STANDS AS A GRAND REMINDER of Kalispell's 19th-century past. This unique, Queen-Anne style home is named after its original owners Sophie and John McIntosh and still reflects the promise and vibrancy of the 1890s.

John McIntosh was born in Canada (of Scottish descent). In 1891, he moved to Kalispell and set up the first hardware store in Kalispell, which he named John McIntosh & Co.

As newlyweds, John and Sophie built their home atop "Knob Hill," a naturally elevated area in town. When the home was completed in 1894, Kalispell looked quite different as houses were few and far between, which afforded tremendous views in every direction.

In fact, the Flathead Herald-Journal reported that the house stood at "the most exalted position in Kalispell." Obviously, much has changed since then, and the view from the McIntosh House is now little more than unremarkably suburban.

Aside from the bygone views, practically all of the other original characteristics of the home remain intact. For example, the house still has its original "upright and wing" layout: a two-story gable on one side and a single-story wing on the other.

The original "fish scale" siding, "wavy" clapboard and decorative wood trim – all painted in delightfully unavoidable colors – reveal hallmarks of the Victorian era.

It's fortunate that not much has been added to or removed from the house in the last 120 years. Which is quite remarkable, considering that McIntosh was a rather ambitious entrepreneur. Yet perhaps McIntosh did not significantly alter the home because he was too busy building and running an opera house.

In 1896, just two years after building this house, he built the McIntosh Opera House on Main Street above his hardware store (where Western Outdoor and Norm's News are now located).

Initially, the opera house was a success and several other businesses set up in the "Opera Block." Although over time, society changed, and so did the need and use of the opera hall. It was no longer exclusively for operas, and served as a roller rink, basketball court, dance hall, boxing ring and rental hall.

In his later years, McIntosh advertised the hall from his house. Folks seeking to rent the hall, could stop by the McIntosh residence or just dial the house phone number: 108L.

Even at the age of 86, McIntosh would answer the phone and handle business regarding the meeting hall from the home. And at the age of 90, after he "retired" as best he could, McIntosh still remained busy tending to the vegetable and flower gardens he kept in the yard.

Unfortunately, Sophie died in 1920 and John died in 1947. Together they raised four children in the home, which remained in the McIntosh family until 1979.

Fortunately, we can still appreciate their original Queen-Anne-style home thanks to McIntosh's entrepreneurial ambitions (which likely kept him preoccupied and away from fussing with the home's design), and the great care that has been provided for the home over the years.

So the next time you're around "Knob Hill," be sure to take a moment and appreciate the McIntosh House – one of the best-kept, original "upright and wing" homes in Kalispell.

McIntosh Opera House

48 MAIN STREET, KALISPELL

IF EVER WALLS COULD TALK...

Basketball. Boxing. Rodeo Dance. Sheridan's Orchestra. The Flathead County Six. The Boneless Wonder. The County Fair. Oil Prospecting. Temperance!

These are a few of the topics the walls of the McIntosh Opera House could mention.

In 1891, Canadian immigrant John McIntosh moved to Kalispell and founded the first hardware store. Later, he built a house in town and then began working on the opera house – just above the location of his hardware store. It is now known as 48 Main Street above Norm's News and the Western Outdoor shops.

Upon completion in 1896, the McIntosh Opera House played a long and varied role in the history of Kalispell and the Flathead Valley. From the 1890s through the 1930s, the McIntosh Opera House was the epicenter of culture in early Kalispell. There was hardly a group, speaker or troupe that did not pass through its doors.

The Opera House is where residents of Kalispell shared ideas, entertained themselves and helped their neighbors. Consequently, the memory of the Opera House is made up of many things.

It is the rally speech of Eugene Debs in 1902, the Socialist candidate for the President of the United States, who passionately casted reform aloft.

It is the box of stationary won by the best lady waltzer on February 2, 1917, showing the pride of community.

It is meeting by the fountain in the early 1920s outside the Kalispell Grand Hotel. And it is the memory of eating "hot-dog sandwiches" while listening to the Somers Male Quartette sing "Land O' the Leal."

Today, much of the original opera house is but a memory. Its shell is intact, but not much else is in its proper, original form. The once grand entrance (a large metal door) on Main Street no longer leads to a grand lobby. And the 90 opera seats installed in 1908, if they could ever be found and replaced, would seat an empty stage.

As the prominence of the opera house waned in the 1930s, a cigarette butt sealed its fate on June 29, 1935. Behind the curtain, some dancers were having a late rehearsal that Friday night. While returning to the set after an early-morning break, one of them tossed a cigarette across the stage.

An intense fire started burning, with flammable gases that became tremendously hot and caused an explosion. A quick-thinking hotel clerk across from the Opera House, called for the fire department. The fire brigade arrived in a flash, and with the help of some rain, the Opera House and the adjacent buildings were saved. However, the centerpiece of the Opera House – the stage – had burned beyond salvaging.

Perhaps mired in the insurance problems afterward – or perhaps to spite the loss – owner John McIntosh never rebuilt the stage. And for the rest of its days, the once glorious "opera house" became a hollow "meeting hall" never reclaiming its poise or grace. Its afterlife found itself as a wrestling and boxing venue, and the occasional site for community discussion.

So, if you pass by the McIntosh Opera House, be sure to appreciate its brickwork, arched windows, and its false front. And while listening to whatever "talk" may still resound, don't overlook the plaque atop the building. For it is a true relic of our modern times, as it reads: "OPERA HOUSE."

Moore-Slack House

404 SECOND AVENUE WEST, KALISPELL

THIS SIMPLE, FRONT-GABLE HOME WAS BUILT BETWEEN 1894-1899 by Cora (Brooks) Moore, a housekeeper, who was just 25 years old. It was remarkable at the time for such a young woman to own her own home – and even more remarkable for her to own without the burden of a mortgage, as she did.

The home was built simple, fit and trim for raising a family. However, the neighborhood left more to be desired. At the time, Cora's neighbors included livery stables, saloons, and "women's boarding houses" (which was then a polite term for "houses of prostitution").

Like many other western towns, Kalispell had its own red-light district and places of pleasure. However, as times changed, the "red lights" near saloons were replaced by the "stained glass" windows of churches, which were built to anchor and reform many once-sultrier neighborhoods in Kalispell and other western towns.

During the early 20th century, getting rid of social vices seemed to be a social and political pastime (if only to put things in their proper place). And while the boarding houses were demolished, and churches sprung up instead, this house stood still – as if refraining from judgment and keeping its own tradition of being a home for hard-working families and those of a more hard-working manner.

In 1901, Claude Jump, who owned a livery stable just about a block away, rented the property. Later, in 1910, Ezra and Catherine Slack purchased the home. It was a retirement home for the Slacks, as Ezra worked hard founding and operating one of Kalispell's notable realty companies.

Ezra and Catherine were auto enthusiasts, which is noteworthy considering that traveling by automobile was a relatively new form of travel in Northwest Montana at the time.

Ezra often shared information about road conditions with fellow motorists of his day. For example, a 1916 newspaper article features his report about the "mud-hole" just over the Lincoln County line on the way to Libby (which by the way, had dried up and caused little fuss as he motored through it).

Times were quite different then, and conversations in the front room of this fine and humble home were full of talk about motoring, news from visiting friends and relatives, and other business of the day.

Unfortunately, Ezra passed in 1918, and Catherine passed in 1924. The home had new owners and new neighbors, yet more or less "kept to itself" and changed rather little. About the same time electricity was added to the home, the original back porch was removed, and a new porch (with Craftsman-style hints) was added to the front.

However, aside from the porch rearrangement, much of the original footprint of the house remains the same. For example, on the inside, a closed staircase still leads up to a pair of cozy bedrooms. And the color scheme it features today is actually similar to the original paint scheme, save for swapping the colors of the siding for the color of the fascia and other variations.

However, judging a house by its paint scheme is much like judging a book by its cover: both can be deceiving. For this humble home could easily be reckoned more like a fortress – one that has withstood drastic social changes during its time and also drastic transformations that tend to plunder historic homes of their history and charm. Fortunately, we can still appreciate this house for its basic design, simple front gable, centered chimney and other signs of an era long ago.

Morgan House

344 SIXTH AVENUE EAST, KALISPELL

THERE'S MORE TO THE HISTORY OF A HOME THAN ITS FAÇADE. Oftentimes, the people who lived there – and their artifacts – can reveal more about history than any façade or painted fascia ever could.

For example, at 344 Sixth Ave. E., across from the Conrad Mansion, sits a stately home known as the "Morgan House" after Franklin M. Morgan, the renowned architect who was the designer and original owner of the home.

Morgan designed the house for himself in 1892, adopting many of the appointments of the Queen Anne style. However, a drastic remodeling in 1924 by the MacDonald family transformed it into the Colonial Revival as it appears now.

Indeed, with Morgan and the MacDonalds, the early documented history of the home and its owners speaks of prominence, accomplishment and respect. It would take a separate book to tell the significance of Morgan's architectural footprint in Montana, and another to tell the gilded history of its later owners.

Yet every house has a story itself. A story seldom told – unless you dig for it.

The current owners, Mitch and Stacy Burgard, certainly treasure the house. They've spent considerable time tending to its maintenance – and learning more about its rich history.

Aside from scrutinizing materials from the archives, Mitch Burgard has also completed other important work to uncover the home's history: he's dug around in the crawl space.

Burgard shared some of the artifacts he found in the crawl-space – artifacts that tell a history often not seen or heard.

For example, Burgard found pieces of the original wallpaper and the original trim work that provide insight into Morgan's taste and aesthetic sensibility.

He also found artifacts that reveal some of the social interactions that took place inside the home. For example, Burgard found a Bridge scorecard with the name "Conrad" written at the top, suggesting that the neighbors from the Conrad Mansion across the street played Bridge here as well (the Conrads' score wasn't too impressive by the way).

Interestingly, Burgard also found various champagne and liquor bottles, matchbooks and a 1919 can of Copenhagen chewing tobacco in the basement. These artifacts tell perhaps a different side of the history of the home.

They suggest that while the parlor hosted prominent guests of early Kalispell, some of home's residents, servants and visitors took to the basement to steal a cigarette or a lick of their favorite libation. It's a seedier side of the home's history – and one we'd likely never guess from its stately appearance above ground.

This also hints to an interesting dichotomy that seems prevalent in the history of the house. For example, in 1902 the home was owned by John Harrington Edwards and his wife Mary. Both were prominent citizens of early Kalispell. Mary was noted by the Kalispell Bee newspaper in 1905 as "the most prominent public benefactor Kalispell has had."

Yet at the same time, their live-in servant and cook, Edward Cooper, was arrested for shooting at a rival who was also courting the affections of Ms. Delilah Sounds.

This house is not only a fine example of early 20th century ideals. It's also a reminder that there's more to a home than just its appearance – and the outward appearance of its owners. One should not judge a house by its jerkinhead gabled roof, its balustrades, columns, or balconies, or its design appointments by one of Montana's most important architects. The Morgan House reminds us that sometimes to better understand the history of a home, you just need to dig a little.

"Old Steel Bridge"

KALISPELL

WITH A BIT OF EMPATHY, IMAGINATION AND A FEW HISTORICAL facts, we can transcend nostalgia. And if we let ourselves slip away from modern-day distractions, and give history an earnest thought, we can discover things we take for granted – things like bridges.

Think for a second: Can you name all the bridges you crossed on a recent drive? When did you last plan your driving route around the conditions at a river crossing? Sure, some bridges may be rather obvious, but many are taken for granted. And if there is any local bridge that has been taken for granted, it is the Old Steel Bridge (formerly known as the "Steel Bridge" or the "Holt Stage Bridge").

In the 1890s, when the bridge was built, many practical matters were still quite troublesome. For example, unlike today, crossing the Flathead River was a time-consuming daily chore and required boarding a cable ferry – both ways. If conditions on the river were bad, the crossing could be perilous – if not impossible.

Back then, crossing the Flathead was a problem, and the Gillette-Herzog Manufacturing Company of Minneapolis was commissioned to engineer a solution. Their solution was a steel "Pratt through truss" bridge erected over the Flathead River in 1894. At the time, it was nothing short of an engineering marvel (and in many ways, it still is).

The bridge was carried by freight train – and then hauled by ox cart – to the site (now just south of Highway 35, along Holt Stage Road).

And from 1894 until 2008, the bridge was in place – a prolonged use for which it was never intended. The bridge was originally designed for pedestrians and horse-carts (the first automobile didn't arrive in Kalispell until about 20 years later). So for the better of 80 years, the bridge suffered under the constant use of much-heavier cars and trucks.

Ultimately, in 2008, the bridge was decommissioned and seemed headed to the salvage yard. That's when a fellow named "Crazy Pete" (known on official documents as Pete Skibsrud) intervened.

Pete was shocked that part of local history would just be sold for scrap. So he put down $15,000 of his own money to buy the century-old, 140-foot long, 22-ton steel bridge – stuck alongside the Old Steel Bridge Fish Access site.

While buying a "rusty old bridge" may seem crazy, Pete may be even crazier because anyone who thought they could find another purpose for the bridge must be insane. Despite Pete's tireless efforts, he has unfortunately been unable to put the bridge to good use, even as something simple, such as part of a walking trail.

Meanwhile, officials are becoming impatient, and have recently pressured Pete to relocate the "unattractive nuisance." Yet, while some forsake the Old Steel Bridge, others are quite aware that it would take volumes of books to tell the history of this "nuisance."

For example, old newspaper articles tell of community picnics at the banks of the Steel Bridge, fishing near its piers, its defiance of raging floods, and even the life-changing car accidents along its span – all of which tell its story and place in local history.

So despite the lore and iconic presence of the bridge, without a plan for the future, it slips closer to demolition every day. And it doesn't take a clairvoyant to see the future: without help, we will lose another landmark of the "pioneer era" of the Flathead Valley.

This article was originally published on August 6, 2013. The "Old Steel Bridge" was sold and dismantled in April, 2014. Artist/blacksmith Jeffrey Funk purchased the bridge and cut the bridge into pieces to re-use in different art and building projects. The Old Steel Bridge is now a lost landmark of the Flathead Valley. Pete Skibsrud tried for years to preserve this landmark, and his efforts should be regarded with the utmost admiration and appreciation.

Peterson House

604 FOURTH AVENUE EAST, KALISPELL

WHEN IT COMES TO BUILDING A HOME, SOMETIMES THE MATERIals used to build it define the home (and its legacy) as much as the people who built it.

For example, consider the home at 604 Fourth Ave. E. in Kalispell. It was the first home to be built on the block, back in 1896 (for a bit of perspective, it's the same year that Utah became the 45th state).

The house was built by Swedish immigrants Olaf Peterson and his wife Johanna. Olaf was a section boss and held other positions with various railroads. Later, Peterson was involved in mining and other pursuits.

It's interesting to note that the Petersons built the home using brick – striking red-orange brick. The home stands out from other houses – and stands at odds with them too. The Peterson House was built of brick, while all other homes built later on the block were made of wood-frame construction. The home also stood at odds with many of its later occupants – especially the ones who ironically worked in the lumber industry.

The Petersons, who built the home and gave this home its namesake, sold it in 1908 to George Millet – a timber dealer.

Millet shortly sold the home to Julius Neils of Portland, Ore., who was a lumberman with dealings throughout the Pacific Northwest. While expanding his lumber enterprise in Montana, Neils sent his son-in-law, Harry Schocknecht, to establish lumberyards in the Kalispell area and elsewhere around Northwest Montana. The Schocknecht family lived in the home until about 1915. The Schocknechts – a lumber family – also lived in this fine brick house.

And perhaps the last resident with lumber affiliations to live in the house was Thomas Gardner, a logging contractor who lived in the home with his family during the 1920s.

The home also served briefly as a parish house for the Trinity Lutheran Church in the neighborhood. And it was also the residence of Dr. Ralph Towne and his wife Marie from 1936 until 1967.

At some point in the early 20th century, renowned Kalispell architect Fred Brinkman designed its newer windows, one of the few modifications that were made to the original 19th-century Victorian shape and design – and its striking red-orange brick exterior. An enclosed porch is perhaps the only other more noticeable addition.

Fortunately, the original brick exterior, with its tall, gabled roof, still stands for us to appreciate as a reminder of one of Kalispell's earliest brick homes – that remains well intact today.

Phillips House

445 FIFTH AVENUE EAST, KALISPELL

THE HOUSE AT 445 FIFTH AVE. E. HAS SEVERAL CHARACTERISTICS that define Kalispell neighborhoods – in a way that may seem deceiving, and distorted by time.

Originally, a small wooden residence stood at the back of this corner lot. It was destroyed by fire in 1910, and the lot remained empty for the better part of three decades, as sometimes happens when calamity strikes.

But sometimes it takes a calamity of greater proportion to make any progress happen. And in this case, widespread drought of the 1920s and the economic depression of the 1930s caused many people to seek refuge in Kalispell. At the time, Kalispell and surrounding areas were faring comparatively well – well enough to even say that Kalispell had a building "bang" (not quite enough to properly call it a "boom") during the 1930s.

Consequently those moving to the area found the hardships of the time somewhat easier to endure, and some even found profit. And it took a bit of both – populace and profit – to transform what was once an overgrown, eyesore lot into a desirable home inspired by the vogue, Tudor Revival home.

Like other Depression-era settlers, Leon and Ella Phillips came to Kalispell in the early 1930s. Leon brought with him vast experience in the automotive business. He worked throughout the borders and corners of Montana as a mechanic, salesman and dealer. After several successful years, he became president of Phillips-Wohlwend Motors, and built this home as his family residence, which was more or less completed in 1938.

The late 1930s was a time of transition (from hardship to hope and not much beyond). It was a time when the "haves" could perhaps afford the $695 price tag for a new 1936 Dodge Rumble Seat Coupe (along with the 6 percent interest typical of most financing arrangements of the day).

Phillips established the auto dealership bearing his name, Phillips-Wohlwend Motors, at 412 Main St. (remembered by some as Big Valley Dodge; and now home to the Kalispell Brewing Company). The location has long been known as an auto dealership, from the day Phillips founded the company and for the better part of nearly four decades.

Yet while his business legacy lasted decades, the Phillips family lived in the home for barely four years. In 1942, they sold the home to Virgil Manion, then president of Manion Motors. And so continued the lineage of home ownership by presidents of auto dealerships. That is, at least until 1956, when the Manions sold the home.

Aside from being owned by auto dealers, the house was home to their families, and frequently open to relatives and guests, as both men and their wives were quite active in community and civic organizations.

Inside and out, this home was a fine adaptation of the Tudor Revival style, yet on a smaller scale. Obvious exterior elements of the Tudor Revival style, which was quite popular in Kalispell at the time, include the stucco siding, the tabbed archway and recessed front door, and the decorative shutters, just to name a few.

Today, the home is fortunately well maintained with a tiled roof and other elements that nod to its original style. And style it had, as it was one of the finer ones built in its day – a time when "rent houses" were less stylish and more common.

While it may seem modest now, if not unremarkable to some, the house was actually quite indulgent for its day, proving that sometimes truly appreciating an historic home takes a bit of discerning "what is now" from "that was then."

Polebridge Mercantile

265 POLEBRIDGE LOOP ROAD, POLEBRIDGE

FEW PLACES WITHSTAND THE FORCES OF CHANGE – AND FEW places remain the same today as they were a century ago. Fortunately, the Polebridge Mercantile is indeed one of those places.

Rambling along Montana Highway 486 from Columbia Falls, time fades with the passing of each of the 35 miles it takes to get to the rough-handed North Fork Valley town of Polebridge. In many ways, the trip defines "off the beaten path."

As time fades, so does your cellphone service, which seems fair, considering that true appreciation of this landmark requires appreciation for its surroundings (and the less distraction from digital encumbrances, the better).

The Polebridge Mercantile stands where wildlife still outnumber residents by the thousands. Electricity has yet to reach the area (and maybe never will, considering the respect of nature and way of life of the dozens of year-round residents).

And while cars have replaced horses and pack animals as the means of travel to the "store," it still remains a bakery, post office, sandwich shop, meeting place, base camp and general store all in one.

Some of the original handiwork and construction can still be seen today, as a quick glance up at the original ceiling rafters above shows some of the hand-hewn wood and tree limbs (some with the bark still on them) that were used.

Sure, you can no longer buy Standard Oil "Red Crown" gasoline anymore. And beverages are no longer kept in iceboxes with ice from the historic icehouse. But despite "progress," when nature calls, you're still using the outhouse, much the same as when it was established in 1912 by brothers William and Jesse Adair who settled at a 160-acre homestead

The Adair brothers completed the store in 1914, and it soon became known as "Adairs." Later the Adair brothers added the outbuildings that are also listed on the historic register as part of the W.L. Adair General Mercantile Historic District.

Their original cabin still stands next to the shop. Although, now it is part of the Northern Lights Saloon with a volleyball net outside, where a vegetable patch likely once was.

And perhaps the only thing that has changed substantially is the name, from "Adairs" to the "Polebridge Mercantile" – which refers to the pole bridge over the nearby North Fork River. Incidentally, William Adair telephoned county officials when the bridge went out in a flood in March of 1932.

Unfortunately, floods, mudslides and stubborn elk herds weren't the only threats and hassles for the mercantile and the surrounding landscape. The Red Bench Fire of 1988 came dangerously close to the establishment, and burned the historic 1922 barn to the ground.

Fortunately, with great help, the store and other buildings were spared and the iconic storefront still stands, which features a false-front or boomtown-style façade. Such façades were used to transform simple gabled buildings of the west and advertise them as a more prominent place of commerce.

Indeed, life in the area surrounding the Polebridge Mercantile can be demanding. It demands the sacrifice of modern convenience and comfort, such as cellular technology and a smooth ride to get there. It demands our respect for a way of life that has long since been forgotten in most other places. And it demands our respect for the past – and commitment to preserving the legacy of the Polebridge Mercantile in the future.

J.E. Rockwood House

835 FIRST AVENUE EAST, KALISPELL

IN THE SHADOWS OF THE HISTORIC FLATHEAD COUNTY Courthouse stands a Craftsman-style home at 835 First Ave. E. It's remarkable as a reminder of early 20th-century Kalispell history in many ways. It's a great example of Kalispell's Craftsman style. And it was the home of lawyer, judge and former Montana state Rep. Joseph E. Rockwood, whose work affected the lives and landscape of the Flathead Valley in many ways.

Undoubtedly, as a judge, Rockwood took his work home with him. And from home, he could see his work; and from work, he could see his home. And due to their proximity, Rockwood likely took his work home with him and must have deliberated the fate of more than a few Kalispell residents inside the home.

Rockwood presided at a time when gambling and vagrancy were garden-variety offenses. Vagrants were often "floated," that is escorted to the Flathead County line and told to leave or face jail time. He also deliberated cases that found a pinball machine was "a gambling device and public nuisance." And some less trivial cases included the condemning of land held by the Belton Mercantile for the new entrance into Glacier National Park.

Rockwood had a passion for law – and horses. He was a member of the Kalispell Saddle Club. And as a testament to his fondness for things equine, the horse barn that he built still stands on the alley of the residence (although converted as a living space now).

But Rockwood's passion for horses did more than shape the outbuilding on this city lot. His passion for law and horses passed on to his son Forrest, one of the two children Rockwood raised with his wife Minnie Saeger, who he married in 1897. Forrest was also a lawyer, and an avid horseman, and was instrumental in expanding horseback riding in the Bob Marshall Wilderness.

The home also hosted some interesting company. Aside from visits from his legal and political circles as a district judge and member of the Montana House of Representatives, Rockwood and his wife were members of various social organizations.

For example, the home was host to the annual Christmas party of The Past Noble Grand Circle in 1940. Rockwood was also a member of the Independent Order of Odd Fellows (and Rockwood's Odd Fellows jacket can be found at the Central School Museum).

Rockwood hired Frederick C. Mercord, a Kalispell contractor, to build the home between 1922 and 1925. Mercord began working as a building contractor in 1908, and bought and sold properties and built several homes in the downtown Kalispell area.

This home features Mercord's handiwork and several of the iconic Craftsman-style elements. For example, below the large, gabled front dormer, a porch spans the front of the home. Like other Craftsman-style homes, this one also plays with symmetry and numbers.

The Rockwood House shows signs of the number three. For example, there are three windows on each side of the front door. And three windows in the gabled front dormer – that has three exposed brackets under the eaves. At the side of the house, there are three sets of windows on each story. And there are three porch columns at each corner.

Also typical of the Craftsman style, the home features hardwood floors and custom "built-ins," including bookcases and a china-hutch.

So the next time you're passing the roundabout at the courthouse, glance over to the east at the Rockwood House. It's a fine example of a Kalispell Craftsman – and a place where many issues of early 20th-century life in the Flathead Valley were likely debated and deliberated.

Ross House

820 THIRD AVENUE WEST, KALISPELL

OFTENTIMES, WHAT MAKES A "LANDMARK" HOME A LANDMARK is plain to see. Whether it's a fancy façade or elements of the Victorian vernacular, the style of such homes may seem striking, or obvious at the least.

However, when it comes to certain homes, their significance may be more difficult to see (even when squinting). And for some homes, their historical importance may be nearly lost among things "erstwhile" and "bygone."

The Ross House, at 820 Third Ave. W. in Kalispell, is a bit of both. Overall, it's a fine example of moderation in the "roaring '20s" – a modest house with a charming vernacular style built between 1920 and 1927.

For example, it's not precisely a cross-gabled Craftsman, but something of a similar "cross-dormered" construction, one that adds living space and style without forsaking economy.

The home also features a full-length front porch. "Front porch homes" were quite a luxury, yet the Ross House exemplifies style without forsaking economy. For example, the porch railings (with the spindles squared at the top and bottom) give the illusion of a denticulated balustrade or dentil molding that typically adorn the cornices of more boastful residences.

Likewise, the stamped concrete block mimics the far more costly stone foundations of larger, more expensive homes as well.

And while the stylistic details and appointments of the home may take a minute or two to spot, the historical significance of the home may seem even less obvious.

The home is the namesake of Lynn Ross and his wife Isabel. In 1928, they rented the home from Mrs. Emma Gregg, who owned the home during the 1920s.

In 1930, Mr. and Mrs. Ross, along with their two daughters, did something that may seem quite strange nowadays: they shared the home with 16-year-old boarder Helen Froese, so she could attend the nearby Flathead County High School.

At the time, many students attended a rural school up to the eighth grade. So for a child to continue their studies, a family would have to make boarding arrangements or move closer to a high school, which was typically located "in town."

Many parents throughout the Flathead Valley faced such a similar dilemma. Some sent their children to board in town, as was likely the case with Ms. Froese. Others managed their farm operations as best they could, and kept "a place in town" so their children could attend school during the "off season" and rented it during the summer.

Some parents sold their farms – and their way of life – to move into town so their children could continue schooling. Nowadays, we have the era of "No Child Left Behind." Back then, some children were just plain "left out" as education was a perishable commodity.

Education was cut short for many children, particularly those without means to board at a place such as the Ross House or the other neighborhood homes that were also rented out for students and their families.

Certainly, the Ross House should be appreciated for its clever-yet-stylish economy. And while education can seem ethereal (especially since we may not see enough of it), it should also be appreciated for its harder-to-see legacy: its place in helping to educate a generation of students in the Flathead Valley.

Rostad House

704 FIRST AVENUE WEST, KALISPELL

THE EARLY 20TH CENTURY WAS A TIME OF GREAT CHANGE IN THE Flathead Valley. For example, when this home was finished, sometime before 1903, the shores of Flathead Lake saw both the passing of company steamboats hauling freight and Kootenai canoes covered with elk skin.

And as always in times of change, some things stay the same. And this fine Queen Anne home, on the corner of First Avenue West and Seventh Street West, stands persistent in its original character and memory of its long-time occupants.

The home was originally owned by C.N. Brown, who in 1905 rented the home to Clarence and Clara Rostad (Clarence was also known as "Rusty"). And from all appearances, things were going well for the Rostads and the house was a home to their family, including a daughter born in 1908.

In 1914, Brown sold the home to James Conlon, owner and operator of the Conlon Mercantile. Conlon was also Rostad's boss for a spell, and continued to rent the home to the Rostad family.

While the Rostad family was fortunate to stay in the home, a near-fatal misfortune would strike that year. A fire broke out on the second floor due to a faulty flue in the chimney. Rostad was burned during the fire and barely made it out alive.

It can be said (without much extension beyond the truth) that he was "burned" again by the fire department since they caused more damage putting out the fire with harsh chemicals. Yet Rostad recovered, and so did the home.

In 1920, after renting the home some 15 years, the Rostad family bought the property, becoming its third owners, and remaining so until 1959.

In 1933, a baby girl joined the Rostad family, along with her older sister and older brother Robert, who operated his radio repair service from the home. Robert advertised a "Standard radio tune-up for only $2" and his proud membership in the "Radio Manufacturers Service" in numerous newspaper advertisements of the day.

The Rostad family remained in the home more than 50 years, leaving an undeniable impression on the neighborhood and early history of Kalispell. Likewise, so did the home itself. Putting the fire aside (perhaps with more ease than Rostad actually could), the home has been an anchor on the corner of this west side neighborhood. Its original structure remains, save for repairs from the fire, and an enclosure around the front porch.

With its persistence, it established a quiet tradition, for the home was a constant, a thing relatively unchanged during fleeting modern times when ways of life would come to pass, and new ones would come (and seemingly go) at break-neck speed.

The home retains much of its original character. Still remaining are the unique floorplan, varied siding patterns, decorative shutters and trim work, and a bay on the side spanning both floors – all hallmarks of the Queen Anne style – and all of which have survived more than a century.

This home with much of its original style – and the legacy of its long-time residents – is a place that has stayed mostly the same over time, despite the vast changes elsewhere throughout Kalispell and the rest of the Flathead Valley.

Sliter House

12 SIXTH AVENUE EAST, KALISPELL

SOMETIMES, IT'S EASY TO OVERLOOK THE DETAILS. BUT ONCE YOU take a little time, details unfold – just like the style and history of a landmark home, such as the "Sliter House" at 512 Sixth Ave. E. in Kalispell. While it may have a familiar-sounding namesake (Sliter's Hardware), its style and history have many details that are often overlooked.

The house is an example of "Victorian Vernacular" style: that is, it has features of several popular Victorian styles, but not enough of any one style in particular whether French Second Empire, Gothic Revival, Italian Villa, Italianate, or a Queen Anne.

Instead, the home has many Victorian elements, such as fine brick and shingle work; a steep, front-facing gable; a section with a mansard roof, and other details – all of which give it an overall Victorian appearance. It is also deep-rooted in Flathead Valley history and tradition.

The house was built in 1897 by Joseph Horn, owner of the Kalispell Mercantile Company (think of it as the 19th-century version of the biggest "shopping mall" in the Flathead Valley). As the Kalispell Mercantile – and Kalispell itself – became more established and successful, Horn built this fine home and helped establish the East Side neighborhood.

In 1905, Horn sold the home to another man who was also becoming more established and successful in the Flathead Valley: Everit Sliter. Sliter arrived in 1889, before Kalispell was founded. Incidentally, Sliter would later do a little "town founding" himself. Like many other early pioneers, Sliter looked toward the future and planned ahead.

During his first year in the Flathead Valley, Sliter worked at the Ramsdell Brothers general store at Egan (a long-lost town of the valley). He spent practically all of his money to purchase land. To "get by," Sliter split rails for fence posts, lived in a root cellar with his dog (where they shared meals from 26 deer) and bartered deerskins for other necessary provisions.

Real estate would serve Sliter quite well. And his 160-acre homestead would later become the town of Bigfork. He platted and filed the original town site of Bigfork in 1902, and the first addition in Bigfork was filed in 1903. After several years at Bigfork, having founded the town, an orchard, a general store, a hotel, and serving as the first postmaster, Sliter and his wife Lizzie decided to move to Kalispell.

In making their move, Sliter bartered. But instead of bartering deerskins as he did in earlier years, Sliter bartered real estate. That is, Sliter and Horn bartered and traded places: Sliter took ownership of Horn's house in Kalispell, and Horn took over Sliter's general store and hotel in Bigfork.

In 1908, the Sliters moved into the house and made it their new home. The house also served as the location for Sliter's real estate business from 1909 until 1917. Undoubtedly, some important, early 20th-century real-estate transactions were created and conducted inside the home.

And the Sliter House is a good reminder that when it comes to architecture, details can be more interesting than making a big impression. And that when it comes to history and traditions, such as bartering real estate, sometimes it's not "what" happened, but "how" things happened, that matters more.

Somers Ice House

THE GREAT NORTHERN HISTORICAL TRAIL, SOMERS ROAD, SOMERS

THROUGHOUT HISTORY, MANY TYPES OF HOUSES HAVE COME and gone. For example, consider the millhouse, the smokehouse, outhouse, and perhaps the most obsolete of them all: the icehouse.

Not long ago, many homes had an icehouse or made use of one. Ringing the "ice man" for delivery was routine. And behemoth icehouses once dotted the Flathead Valley and the Great Northern Railway once had three icehouses in Kalispell and several others in Whitefish.

Today, most icehouses are gone. However, just north of the entrance of The Great Northern Historical Trail entrance on Somers Road stands the Somers icehouse. It's a fine relic of a bygone era. After wondering what it is, many folks wonder why an icehouse would be located so far away from the lake (or anything else for that matter).

Judging by its current location, the Somers icehouse may seem peculiar. It stands in a corner of the Sliter's lumberyard along the edge of a walking/biking trail. That's because the bustling railroad tracks and lumberyard that once surrounded it are no longer there.

In 1901, local entrepreneur John O'Brien struck a deal with James J. Hill, the Great Northern Railway tycoon, to build and run a railroad spur line and sawmill in Somers, named after George Somers, an executive of the operation.

The sawmill provided lumber and much-needed railroad ties for the expansion of the Great Northern Railway. Likewise, the Somers Lumber Company also provided ice for hauling perishable goods and use on passenger cars.

Ice was harvested from the lake usually in late January and kept in the icehouse year round. To keep ice cold – especially in the summer when it was needed most – the icehouse was designed with several deceptively simple features.

For example, there are two layers of wood siding. One layer of wood siding runs diagonally along the side of the icehouse. This layer is covered by another layer of horizontal wood siding. Together, these two layers provide strength and insulation to the walls.

The walls were three-foot thick and filled with sawdust to provide even more insulation. And this ice house had no shortage of sawdust, since it was in the middle of the Somers Lumber Company – the largest sawmill in the Flathead Valley at the time, producing about 600,000 railroad ties per year for the growing railroad.

The second-story door may seem oddly out of place. However, it was used to load ice down into railroad freight cars, and later special "reefer" or refrigerator cars. This was dangerous work and falling and freezing were not uncommon tragedies.

Also, the two cupolas atop the roof aren't just for decoration. They are an integral part of a venting system designed to let warm air draft out and help keep the ice from melting.

While the icehouse was well built and worked well, history would alter its utility.

By 1930, the introduction of electric refrigeration altered the need for natural ice. The use of the General Electric, the Frigidaire, the Kelvinator and other electric refrigerators spread during 1930 through 1960. And the icehouses across the nation soon became obsolete.

About the same time, expansion of the Great Northern Railway had run its course and a half million railroad ties were no longer needed every year.

The sawmill was shuttered in 1949. Since then, the Somers icehouse has survived a few real estate transactions and devious plans of more ambitious utility. Luckily, this relic of life in a different era still sits quietly in place – and remains one of the very few icehouses left.

Waggener & Campbell Funeral Home

228 SECOND STREET WEST, KALISPELL

BEFORE THE 20TH CENTURY, THE DEATH OF A LOVED ONE WAS typically a dour, private affair, held at the home.

However, the "Gilded Age" and the "Gay Nineties" (the 1890s) sparked change and progression – including how Americans handled the passing of loved ones. From corsages, to chapels, to caskets, funerals became increasingly more of an open, public event for expressing respect and homage.

So when James E. Waggener left Oregon and came to Kalispell in 1905, and assumed the operations of retiring undertaker Nelson Willoughby, the original location at 134 West Second St. was quite suitable. Within a few years, however, the modest two-room location would seem crowded – and quite small for Waggener's big ideas.

To accommodate changes in society – and suit his business ambitions – Waggener had to expand. So he commissioned one of Kalispell's early builders, Caesar Haverlandt (who built a few buildings in Kalispell listed on the National Historic Register).

Haverlandt completed the building in 1913. It was designed to accommodate Waggener's growing business, which was considerably more than just undertaking and included funeral arrangements, transportation, casket sales, embalming and more. And for its time, the building was "state-of-the-art," with a spacious showroom and equally accommodating chapel, and the only receiving vault in the area.

In 1916, Waggener's son Elton was awarded his embalmer's license. That same year, Waggener would announce his candidacy for coroner promising "the best service possible for the least amount of expense." He won and served as coroner of Flathead County for the next twelve years.

Waggener's business and profession seemed to be on the up. But on August 3, 1919, his son Elton "died of a toxicity resulting from his profession as an undertaker" having contracted a fatal illness while carrying out his mortuary duties – much like his father, whose business he would have likely inherited.

Aside from the grave misfortune, the building continued to serve Waggener's steady business quite well. Waggener's daughter Geneva later married Harry H. Campbell. Waggener then partnered with his son-in-law and they formed the Waggener & Campbell Funeral Home, the namesake of the building. Together, their father-and-son enterprise continued to succeed and they relocated to a more modern space at 525 Main St. in 1929.

Since then, the building has been converted to accommodate other businesses. And like other buildings, historical structures are preserved well – or get trounced as the decades pass.

Regrettably, some of the original charm of this building has been "blemished" by renovations and repairs. But overlooking things such as the electrical conduits, vents and utilities, the building still shows much of its original pride.

Most of the original brickwork remains solid. And while other original elements may no longer be intact, they are still recognizable. Likewise, the building was originally intended as a funeral home with accommodations for the funeral director's family, and has long since been a dry cleaning business with apartments above.

Yet the funerals that were held here are an inextricable part of local history. Perhaps that's why there's something about the Waggener & Campbell Funeral Home building, its location, and its seemingly stuck-in-time lingering. It's the kind of place where standing on the corner seems to take you back in time (as far back in local history as your imagination can take you).

Walker Residence

540 SECOND AVENUE WEST, KALISPELL

"ONE OF THE HANDSOMEST DWELLING HOUSES IN THE CITY," declared the Kalispell Bee newspaper in 1903. Indeed the Walker Residence was – and in so many ways, still is quite a handsome dwelling.

The home was built by Cassuis McCarty for one of Kalispell's pioneering citizens of prominence, James Wiltse Walker: as in James W. Walker, former school trustee, Kalispell city councilman, Flathead County clerk and recorder, Montana state treasurer and commissioner of Montana Lands and Investments.

Like other pioneers, Walker came to the Flathead Valley in 1892, as news of the promising "railroad town" spread. Walker was originally from Oshkosh, Wis. And after completing studies at Northwestern University School of Pharmacy, he came to the Flathead Valley and operated drug stores in Columbia Falls and Kalispell.

In 1903, the house was completed and became the stately home to Walker, his wife Blanche and their daughter Phyllis.

Aside from being one of "Kalispell's fathers," Walker was an early automobile enthusiast. In retrospect, he had a seemingly odd relationship with all things driving. For example, the residence was one of the first to have an automobile parked outside. His daughter Phyllis was reportedly the first child in Kalispell who learned how to drive. Coincidentally, Walker unfortunately died of a heart attack in 1951 – while standing in line to renew his driver's license, at age 84.

The Walkers defined the home and created its original charm and character. However, they only lived in the home a few years. In 1908, Clifford B. Harris, who was then president of the Kalispell National Bank, purchased the home.

In 1914, John Hogl, of the Kalispell Malting and Brewing Company, moved in and lived in the home for several years as well.

In 1920, Sarah Ingraham bought the home. She is the widow of Sheriff Ingraham – who was a lawman at a time when telegraphs and patrol wagons were used for saloon robberies, coin forgeries, murders and other deeds committed by early 20th-century outlaws and miscreants.

Ingraham converted the home and operated a popular boarding house from 1920 to 1946 – during some of the most trying times in American history, including the Great Depression and World War II.

One of Ingraham's classified ads from 1931 read: "FOR RENT – Rooms with board. 540 2nd Avenue West, phone 491L." The ad reads more like an artifact of a bygone era when phone numbers were four digits or less. And "board," meaning the table or board upon which food was served, made the arrangement quite attractive, especially considering the economic hardships of the day.

In 1964, the home became a single-family residence again. And it is suspected that several hardware items originally installed by the Walkers, and some of the boarders' effects were sold during a rummage sale held in the basement in March 1968.

Fortunately, plenty of the original charm and architectural elements remain for us to appreciate. For example, this classic, double-gabled Queen Anne style home still has its center chimney, which is notably flanked by scalloped roof shingles, similar to the ones adorning the fascia along the gables. The semi-circular windows at each of the gables are also unique. Even the original foundation is notable, as it was made from local rock and stone.

Inside there were originally nine rooms, including a reception hall, servant's room, pantry, laundry room and a fruit room. Other interior appointments included six closets, picture molding, chair railing and plate railing in the dining room.

Indeed, the Walker Residence is a good home for admiring the Queen Anne style, or imagining the lives of prominent early 20th-century residents, or conjuring the busy lives of boarders who lived in the house during three of the most trying decades in American history.

Weberg House

329 FIFTH AVENUE EAST, KALISPELL

THE HOUSE AT 329 FIFTH AVE. E. IN KALISPELL IS THE NAMESAKE of its former owners Peter and Rena Weberg. The Webergs bought the home in 1916 and held it until 1966 when Rena passed in 1966, at the age 93.

It makes sense that Peter Weberg, Kalispell's city treasurer for 29 years, would choose such an efficient, sensible house to call home.

But aside from honoring its past owners, and its simplicity of design, the home should also be appreciated for its controversy – and rebelliousness.

For example, the house always stood in the same spot – but has been in two different places. Kalispell carpenter William Williscroft started building the house in 1891, when Kalispell was part of Missoula County. Williscroft finished construction in 1893, when Kalispell became part of the newly established Flathead County. So, technically speaking, the first nail was hammered in Missoula County, while the last nail was set in Flathead County.

As for the house itself, it is perhaps as simple as simple gets: a one-story, hipped roof house with one center chimney and two windows on each side. Yet therein the simplicity lies the controversy.

At the time the house was built, in the late Victorian era, the prevailing architectural styles could be best described as elaborate and decorative – inspired largely by things of emotion and romance.

Yet, there was opposition to popular sentiments, particularly among those who embraced simplicity and utility over things gaudy, fanciful – meretricious even. And there is perhaps no better example of a house in Kalispell that defied those popular notions of yesteryear more abruptly and more contrarily.

Arguably, Williscroft built this house as an "architectural slap in society's face." Except for the front porch (which was remodeled in the 1950s), practically every aspect of the house contradicted the popular, ostentatious architectural styles of the time.

It was as if Williscroft aimed to declare his contempt for things typically Victorian in building this house. For example, typical Victorian rooflines had many gables, valleys and chimneys. Yet, Williscroft built a basic hipped roof – with just one centered chimney.

And unlike typical Victorian homes, which boast ornate windows of nearly every number and style, Williscroft made the simplest of design choices: two rectangular windows on every side. And while stylish homes of the era seemed to feature wooden shingles of nearly every shape and size (the more peculiar, the better), Williscroft again chose the opposite. For underneath the current stucco veneer stands the original brick walls – perhaps the most utilitarian form available, superior to only mere sod and cob.

And in many ways, the house remains as rebellious now as it was then. In our modern era of the reigning "open floor plan," this simple, four-square cottage may seem backward, confused and obstructed with its center-hall fireplace and chimney. Thus, the Weberg House should be appreciated for its long-standing simplicity and its rebelliousness – both then and now.

MADE IN
MONTANA®
USA

Acknowledgments

This book was by no means a solitary endeavor. It is the product of much-appreciated help, support, and encouragement from so many folks. Specifically, I would like to acknowledge the vision and continued support of Lance Fahrney and Kellyn Brown of the Flathead Beacon newspaper during the year it took to write each of these weekly articles.

I am grateful for the assistance of Diana Carson, Nancy Christenson, Sandra (Lohse) Seiser, and the encouragement of everyone who has taken a moment to tell me how much they appreciate the "Landmarks" column.

I would also like to thank Diana Carson, Kay Burt, and the staff of the Flathead Community College Continuing Education Program for their encouragement, which was offered at just the right moments.

Of course, I am also indebted to the many residents and property owners who have welcomed me, and shared their knowledge and appreciation of history with me. Without them, I certainly would have fewer stories to share.

With much appreciation,
Jaix Chaix
Lakeside, Montana